5-MINUTE SKETCHING
LANDSCAPES

A RotoVision book

Published in 2017 by Search Press Ltd.
Wellwood, North Farm Road
Tunbridge Wells
Kent, TN2 3DR

Reprinted 2018

This book is produced by
RotoVision, an imprint of the Quarto Group,
The Old Brewery, 6 Blundell Street,
London N7 9BH, United Kingdom.
T (0)20 7700 6700
www.QuartoKnows.com

ISBN: 978-1-78221-591-2

Publisher: Mark Searle
Editorial Director: Isheeta Mustafi
Commissioning Editor: Emily Angus
Editor: Nick Jones
Junior Editor: Abbie Sharman
Cover Design: JC Lanaway
Page Design: JC Lanaway

MIX
Paper from
responsible sources
FSC® C016973
www.fsc.org

Image credits

Front and back covers: Virginia Hein
Opposite: Virginia Hein

5-MINUTE SKETCHING
LANDSCAPES

Super-Quick Techniques for Amazing Drawings

VIRGINIA HEIN

SEARCH PRESS

Contents

Chapter 3
FOCUS ON LANDSCAPE ELEMENTS 68

Chapter 4
TAKE IT FURTHER 96

Introduction

WHEREVER YOU LIVE – whether in an urban neighbourhood in a large city, or a small town or rural area – there will be some kind of landscape – even just a city park or a back garden – where you can find a view that is like no other, find a sense of nature.

Everyone has a mental picture when they hear the word 'landscape'. In this book, we will consider a wide variety of landscapes and how to approach sketching them. A landscape includes all the elements of nature – the landforms of mountains, canyons and plateaus as well as shorelines – and the character of the landscape in every region shapes our sense of place.

One of the interesting things about a landscape is that while the landforms – those mountains and canyons – don't move much, what we see and experience changes constantly with the season, the weather, the time of day. This is what makes landscape sketching exciting – and challenging!

Something I especially love about sketching landscapes is that there is always a mood. We respond emotionally to the character of the place we're observing, and the effects of weather and light. When you can feel a mood in the landscape you're observing – turbulent or calm – it brings life and energy to your landscape sketch, allowing you to express emotion with each mark, with every choice of tone and colour.

Why five-minute landscape sketching? Perhaps not every sketch you see in this book was done in five minutes, but the most important decisions you will make in your sketch happen in those first five minutes! Being able to capture the essence of a scene quickly is so valuable, whether you have just a few minutes, or more time later to develop your sketch. Have you ever spent hours on a drawing or painting only to think, 'I started this all wrong'? I certainly have! So let's start by looking at those crucial initial decisions.

Virginia Hein

See the big picture

Quickly sketching a landscape and capturing a sense of place begins with two important things: seeing and selecting. These are the keys to making quick, confident decisions, so you can 'cut to the chase' in your sketch. They are also key to composing a dynamic sketch. Composition – the overall design of your sketch – is what invites the viewer's eye into your image and holds it there. In this first chapter, we'll explore the visual language an artist uses to swiftly communicate a dynamic sketch. Training your eye, as well as training yourself to trust your eye – that's how you confidently jump into capturing the landscape in just five minutes.

Left To show the way this ornate building seems to emerge from surrounding foliage, I simplified foliage shapes with quick grey washes, and splashed on warm yellow for contrast.

Left **Virginia Hein, *Los Angeles Arboretum Thumbnails*, Arcadia, California, USA, 2015.**
With loose washes, pencil and gouache, I aimed to simplify details of the cottage and emphasise the lush foliage around it, and a panorama view across the lake.

Below **Virginia Hein, *Views of the Golden Gate Bridge*, San Francisco, California, USA, 2017.**
The Golden Gate Bridge is an icon of San Francisco, so I wanted to explore sketching it in different ways. I was intrigued by how the land mass interacted with the bridge.

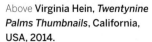

Above **Virginia Hein, *Twentynine Palms Thumbnails*, California, USA, 2014.**
Small studies on a winter afternoon in the Mojave Desert, exploring different formats of the same scene.

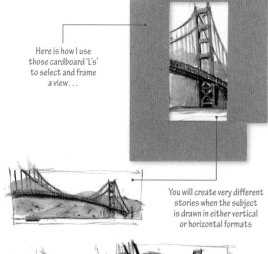

Here is how I use those cardboard 'L's' to select and frame a view...

You will create very different stories when the subject is drawn in either vertical or horizontal formats

Choose the story you want to tell

You discover an inspiring landscape. As you look around, the possibilities of what to sketch can seem overwhelming. Start with selecting your subject; exploring the place and looking at the landscape from different points of view. Then hone in on what really interests you.

Tips to get you started

1 **Take time to really see** When you come to a place you want to sketch, walk around and see what there is to discover. The notion of quick sketching might suggest starting to draw as fast as you can. However, the most valuable thing you can do as you begin is not to draw anything; just spend some time looking.

2 **Discover a point of view** I have a favourite tool – a pair of cardboard 'L's' that I use as an adjustable 'viewfinder'. Just like a camera's viewfinder, it really helps me to hone in and focus on what I find most interesting in a landscape. As I move the viewfinder around the scene, it helps me focus my attention and select an interesting point of view. The viewfinder is also a great way to experiment with seeing how much of the scene you want to include; do you want to capture a sense of the 'big picture' that encompasses a large portion of the landscape, or hone in on a close-up view?

3 **What do you notice?** There's a lot to take in when you observe a landscape – not just the physical landscape, the terrain and the trees, but also more transient things like the light, the weather, the season, the time of day. All these things affect what you see and how you feel about a place at that moment. Capturing a scene isn't just about recording the unchanging 'facts' of a landscape, but observing those more fleeting aspects of nature.

4 **Find your format** The word 'landscape' suggests a horizontal format, but does your sketch have to be horizontal? Definitely not! Another way to use a viewfinder is to play with format, and notice how a vertical format may give you a very different idea about the scene compared to the more usual horizontal shape.

5 **Observe carefully, sketch freely!** Once you have taken time to really observe your scene, and have selected your view, dive in! Quick sketching is a great way to practise interpreting a scene, using suggestion rather than trying to spell out in detail what you see. If you're using a viewfinder to select your scene, now is the time to put it away and let your eye and imagination fill out the picture as you sketch.

Find your horizon line

We generally think of the horizon as the point where the sky appears to meet the land or sea below. It creates an anchor in our visual world. Similarly, the horizon line in landscape art works as an anchor in a picture. Once you find it in a scene, that becomes the foundation of your sketch – even if it's hidden!

Tips to get you started

1 **Find your eye level** The term 'horizon line' is pretty much synonymous with 'eye level'. When you view a scene, you perceive that point where land and sky meet to be exactly the point you see when you're looking straight ahead. It's as if you could draw a line parallel to the ground from your eye to the horizon. The interesting thing is that your perception of that line often changes as you change levels; as you sit down, or climb a hill, the horizon line still appears at your eye level. This is important because it becomes the major point of reference in your sketch for scale and distance.

2 **Anchor your sketch** Unless you're looking at an open plain or out at the ocean, the horizon line may be obscured by trees, buildings or other features. So, you need to visualise a virtual horizon line in front of you. Once you find that line in the landscape, you can choose where to place it in your sketch. It's a good practice to visualise it on your paper, even if it won't appear in your final sketch.

3 **Raise your horizon line** Where you choose to place the horizon line in your sketch is a pivotal decision. Planting that horizontal line in the middle of the page will tend to visually divide your image in half. The funny thing is that we commonly tend towards symmetry without thinking much about it, but it's generally the least interesting way to compose a picture. Where you place that line is all about what you want to emphasise. If you raise the horizon line high in the sketch, notice how it puts your attention on the ground plane.

4 **Bring it low** On the other hand, if you want to emphasise a dramatic sky, for instance, try lowering the horizon line in your sketch. Notice how it changes the emphasis and the feeling of the sketch.

5 **An ocean view... or a road** If you have the opportunity to look out at an ocean view, you can clearly see how your eye level finds that horizon line in front of you. I began sketching as a passenger on open roads some years ago, something I enjoy in part because I can often see that horizon line clearly ahead of me, and how it orients my perception of scale and distance in the same way an ocean view does.

Above left **Shari Blaukopf, *Across the Pond*, Baie d'Urfé, Montreal, Canada, 2014.**
By raising the horizon line very high in this sketch, Shari directs the eye to life in the pond and the beautiful surface reflections.

Above right **Virginia Hein, *Highway 72 to Arizona*, Southern California, USA, 2011.**
Passenger sketching on a large, flat, desert expanse allowed me to clearly see the horizon line, and how the road converged to the centre.

Left **Virginia Hein, *Storm Clouds*, Mojave Desert, California, USA, 2010.**
Here I wanted to emphasise the drama of the storm clouds hovering over the Mojave Desert, so the horizon line is placed very low.

Left **Tom Hoffmann**, *October Colour*, Methow Valley, Washington, USA, 2014.
Tom captures these lovely autumn trees with just the essential shapes. An effective combination of hard and soft edges conveys the feeling of some wind and weather.

Think large shapes first and get those onto paper so you can see the composition

Below **Virginia Hein**, *Rose Garden Thumbnails*, La Canada, California, USA, 2014.
Sketching the frame helped me compose the shapes in these thumbnail sketches, changing the scale and placement of the elements in each.

Below **Virginia Hein**, *Rose Garden Colour Study*, La Canada, California, USA, 2014.
In this sketch I began with large watercolour shapes; I wanted to show the contrast between the structure of the gazebo and the organic shapes in the trees and the foliage.

Squint at the scene and you will see the light and dark contrasting shapes. Simplify your composition by observing what is most distinctive and important and extracting the essence of the scene you are sketching.

See the shapes

The key to quick sketching is learning to see your subject not just as specific objects, but as shapes. When you can see the world in shapes, you'll begin to take control of your sketches! It isn't that you stop seeing your subjects – trees, a mountain, a human being – rather that you see them also as a combination of shapes, fitting into a world of shapes and forms like a shifting puzzle.

Tips to get you started

1 **Practice the 'artist's squint'** A great technique for seeing shapes in your subject is the time-honoured 'artist's squint'. When you squint your eyes, they go slightly out of focus, meaning you see less detail. It's easy to be distracted by all the detail in a scene; practising this technique helps you see the large shapes. As you squint, you let less light into your eye, which makes you less aware of colour. Suddenly you will see strong contrasts of light and dark – shapes. Don't squint at your sketch, however; just notice how squinting at your subject helps you see shapes and compose your sketch.

2 **Simplify!** When you see the large shapes in your subject, it helps you to simplify your composition, to understand what you want to emphasise. The goal here is to 'distil' what you are seeing – to see what's most important so that you can 'extract the essence' from the scene into your sketch. Simplifying is different from generalising; observe what is most distinctive about the scene you're sketching.

3 **Draw a frame** When you look through a viewfinder, you're framing a view – selecting a chunk of nature that's interesting to you. It lets you see the scene in terms of composition: how all the elements are arranged. Drawing a frame on your page does the same thing; you start with a large shape that helps you see the boundaries of your composition.

4 **Think in shape language** Learning to see shapes is a bit like learning a language, and every language has its own vocabulary. When we see shapes we see edges, which can be hard or soft (sometimes called 'lost edges'). Shapes can be geometric, with sharp lines and edges, or organic, with less defined, biomorphic forms found in nature. You begin to master a language when you can think in that language. Mastering shape language helps you communicate your landscape subject quickly!

5 **Large shapes first** If you find that you struggle with drawing too many elements in your sketch, and those elements seem to be competing for attention, it helps to think 'large shapes first'. If you can quickly get down a few large shapes, you can see the composition – the arrangement of your page – immediately. Then, it's a matter of choosing the most important details to communicate, and letting the rest go!

Find your focus

Something attracts you to a scene, and that becomes the focus of your sketch – the 'centre of interest' or 'focal point', drawing the viewer's eye to the thing that you are most interested in. A dynamic composition will generally have a strong focal point, and lead the eye to it in a variety of interesting ways.

Tips to get you started

1 **Notice what grabs your attention** Sometimes you can get so enthralled by a landscape that you work to capture it without thinking too much about what you want to focus on (I've done it!). Pay attention to what it was that first caught your eye. Do you want to make this the centre of interest in your sketch?

2 **Choose the star** Once you establish the focal point, let that be the 'star' of the sketch. Especially when you are quick sketching a landscape, it really helps to recognise what interests you most. You might have more than one area of interest, which can create an interesting, dynamic tension, but let one play a dominant role.

3 **Bring in the supporting players** Let all the other areas of the sketch play supporting roles. Areas around the focal point might lead your eye towards it, or balance the focal point in an interesting way. A road in a landscape leads you to a destination, and it can be direct or indirect, a smooth or a bumpy ride. In the same way, lines and shapes can create paths towards the focal point. Consider how the elements of line, shape or colour can support what interests you most in the sketch.

4 **Direct the eye with contrast** Our eyes are attracted by contrast, whether it be contrasting values of light and dark, sharp edges and surface textures, or contrasting colours. Wherever you have the strongest contrast in a sketch, you have a focal point. Contrasts stand out in a sketch and pull the eye like a magnet!

5 **Be selective** Most of all, the skill of quick sketching is about making choices – you can't include everything, especially with limited time. Part of the art of the sketch is having a clear idea of what you want to focus on, and knowing how much to include. With practice, you'll learn to make quick decisions, and trust them!

Above **Virginia Hein,** *Downhill View*,
Los Angeles, California, USA, 2017.
Another view I sketch often as a passenger – the
downtown Los Angeles skyline seen from the
hills above. The road seems to point like an
arrow to the skyline. I offset the skyline focal
point with the car in the foreground for balance.

Below **Tom Hoffmann,** *Ballston Beach*,
Cape Cod, Massachusetts, USA, 2015.
Tom focuses our attention on that rainbow-
coloured umbrella with the dramatic contrast
of deep shadow in the background.

Below **Virginia Hein,** *Griffith Observatory
in January*, **Los Angeles, California, USA, 2011.**
This is a view I've sketched often, a Los Angeles
landmark that sits high on a hill. I focused on
the way the road zigzags up to the Observatory,
and how that line directed my eye.

Below Virginia Hein, *Afternoon Panorama*,
Los Angeles, California, USA, 2009.
I was far enough away to see two Los Angeles
landmarks: Griffith Observatory and, to the left,
the Hollywood sign. In a panoramic view, you
might have several focal points, but it works best
to make one dominant. Here, I wanted to focus
more on the Observatory.

Our eyes are attracted to
areas of strong contrast. The
bright colours on the umbrella
pull the eye like a magnet.

Practise an awareness
of how light and dark
can create a sense
of balance

Look for pattern
of light and dark

Left Virginia Hein, *Observing Light in Echo Park*, Los Angeles, California, USA, 2016.
In this little monochromatic watercolour study I focused on seeing the patterns of light as much as I was seeing the 'objects' – bridge, trees, birds and so on.

Right **Gabriel Campanario, *Trinidad Beach State Park*, California, USA, 2013.**
Patterns of light sparkle across the water's surface, and convey a feeling of flowing movement.

Below right **Virginia Hein, *Arboretum Notan Study*, Palm Tree, Arcadia, California, USA, 2015.**
I used ink and brush pen to quickly find patterns of light and dark. This meant making choices – which areas to push towards light, and which towards dark – trying to maintain an interesting harmony between the two.

Below **Virginia Hein, *Griffith Observatory View*, Los Angeles, California, USA 2013.**
On a cloudy day, I found the brightest lights were in the foreground buildings and foliage, creating paths of light in the composition.

Notice the light

A wonderful thing about landscape sketching is that you're observing not only the physical, unchanging aspects of the scene – the hills, rocks, trees and so on – but also light. Light is what reveals all of these natural forms in the landscape to you. It can shift in the flash of a moment, with the movement of a cloud or a sudden change in the weather.

Tips to get you started

1 **Look for pattern** We generally think of pattern as an arrangement of repeating forms – everything in nature has pattern. Notice how light reveals patterns in the landscape – like the way groves of trees with masses of foliage create a visual pattern of light and shadow, or the way roofs of buildings may dot a landscape. In a more close-up view, light may shimmer through the dark branches and foliage of a tree, creating an interesting pattern. Reflections in water may repeat the pattern of trees or other nearby objects. Seeing patterns of light in the landscape really helps you quickly compose your sketch.

2 **Create a path** You often see paths or roads in a landscape – and your eye travels those paths. Here's where you want to use the 'artist's squint'. Notice as you blur your vision slightly that you start to see areas of light and shade more clearly. As you translate these areas into your sketch, see if you can form patterns of light for the eye to follow.

3 **Simplify the forms** Very importantly, notice how forms in the landscape simplify when you squint at them; the lights and darks stand out much more distinctly. This is a great way to see how you can arrange forms in your sketch. Follow the shapes of light and dark that you see.

4 **Push the values** Often with quick sketching there's a tendency to hold back, or to stop short of a full range of light to dark. Instead, see if you can quickly commit to where you want dark areas in your sketch, and establish those immediately. 'Pushing the values' means seeing the drama of light and dark in the landscape, and interpreting that boldly in your sketch – from the lightest light to the darkest dark.

5 **Look for harmony of light and dark** There is a Japanese term for the harmony of light and dark: 'Notan', literally 'light-dark balance'. The great landscape painters of China and Japan understood this; in fact the subject of those lovely ink paintings was most frequently harmony in the natural world. As you quickly compose your sketch, practise an awareness of how light and dark can give a sense of balance.

Sketch the shadows

When you are observing light, of course you're also seeing shadows. The shape, colour and density of shadows changes with the weather, the season and the time of day. Just as the effects of light on the landscape are changing all the time, so are the shadows. I like to observe shadows even when I'm not sketching; I think it's a good habit to notice how varied and changeable shadows really are in all kinds of weather and every season.

Tips to get you started

1 **Notice different shadows** There are basically two kinds of shadows. Form shadows define the shape of an object, revealing the surface and textures of the object as they wrap around the side that is away from the light source. Cast shadows are usually darker and more distinct, being the shadows that fall where an object blocks the light.

2 **How's the weather?** Certainly a bright sun in a cloudless sky will cast a stronger shadow than you see on a cloudy day. Depending on the atmosphere, light will be sharply defined or soft and diffused, and so will the shadows.

3 **What time is it?** Time of day as well as the season affect the size and shape of shadows. Early in the morning and late in the afternoon you'll see long cast shadows when the sun is nearer the horizon. At midday, of course, cast shadows are much shorter. The effects of the seasons are more subtle (depending on your latitude); you may see shorter shadows in the summer, when the sun arcs higher in the sky.

4 **See the shapes of shadows** Practise seeing the patterns of dark and light in the landscape created by light and shadows. If you focus on drawing just the 'things' in the landscape, you may miss the drama of shadow and light. Try sketching the shadow shapes first, noticing how they may appear to overlap the objects. Notice, too, where shadows appear sharp and defined and where they soften at the edges.

5 **Look for reflected light** We usually think of shadows as being not only darker than the surrounding area but 'cooler' in colour. This depends on the light source, and the colours in the environment. Warm, golden sunlight tends to produce shadows that are the opposite (the complement) to the light – a cool blue. But, if the shadow is falling on a 'warm' colour surface, you may see a warm colour glow. Atmosphere, time of day – so many things can affect how you perceive shadows. Keep observing!

Left **Shari Blaukopf, *Warm Cold Blue*, Pointe Claire, Quebec, 2015.** Shari paints dramatic shadow shapes in the snow in cool tones of blue-violet.

Below **Virginia Hein, *Arboretum Fig Tree*, Arcadia, California, USA, 2015.** The play of light and shadow was striking on this spreading fig tree. I wanted to show how light reveals texture in the foliage, and creates a strong pattern of shadow beneath the canopy.

Above **Virginia Hein, *Descanso Gardens in August*, La Canada, California, USA, 2016.** In this little gouache study I tried to show the striking contrast between the 'hot' yellow greens of foliage and the cool, violet shadow on a summer afternoon.

Right **Virginia Hein, *Sunset over the Mountains*, Mojave Desert, California, USA, 2014.** I tried to quickly catch the last light in the desert directly with watercolour. I was struck by the light of the setting sun on the mountain at right, and the contrast of violet shadows.

21

See where a line can take you

A line by definition is the path of a moving point – it takes us from one place to another. 'Path' is a useful word here, because that is exactly how it works in a sketch – it leads the eye. Besides moving the eye in any direction, line can describe the edges and boundaries of objects; show pattern and texture, and depending on how the mark is made, show mood and emotion.

Tips to get you started

1 **Describe edges** You will sometimes hear it said that 'there are no lines in nature', but lines are certainly useful to artists to show the edges and boundaries of things, one against the other. Experiment with different kinds of line to describe different things; a line to describe the edge of a leaf might be very different from the line you make to describe the pattern of foliage or the surface of a tree trunk.

2 **Follow contours** Another word for a line that describes the edge of a form is a contour. A contour line follows the form of objects. When you are carefully observing nature as you draw, your line starts to take on the infinite variation that you are seeing.

3 **Move the eye** A line is a powerful tool to direct the eye. Notice the effect that different lines can have on the viewer. A composition of mainly vertical lines might be like walking through a forest of tall trees – there's a sense of stability and strength. Horizontal lines, like a calm sea, tend to have a restful effect. Diagonal lines tend to be dynamic and exciting, and create movement in a composition. Notice how straight lines can have a very different effect in your drawing than soft, undulating, curved lines.

4 **Show pattern and texture** Depending on the tool you use, and the way you vary your lines – short, long, rough or smooth, fine and delicate, or heavy and bold – line can describe all kinds of surface textures and patterns. With quick sketching, it can be very effective to simply suggest pattern and texture with an economy of marks.

5 **Respond with feeling** Drawing is a way to engage all of the senses. Feel how your pencil or pen is an extension of your hand, and notice the connection between your hand, the tool and the paper. When you feel that connection, you aren't just making a picture of something; you are responding to what you see and feel in the marks or lines you make.

Contour lines on forms like tree branches can show volume as well as direction

Above **Virginia Hein,** *Parking Lot Tree*, **La Canada, California, USA, 2010.**
I parked under this spreading tree, very grateful for its shade. I could see the way lines wrapped around undulating branches, describing the contours.

Below **Virginia Hein,** *The High Country*, **Eastern Sierras, California, USA, 2010.**
Approaching the Tioga Pass to Yosemite felt a bit like climbing to heaven; the road is an indirect passage up into high, snowy mountains.

Above **Pat Southern-Pearce,** *Furrowed Fields*, **near St. Ives, Cornwall, 2000.**
Pat creates direction and texture in this lively sketch with fountain pen, palette knife and brush, and a very sensitive hand.

Below **Laura Murphy Frankstone,** *Rock Formations on Whitesands Bay*, Wales, 2016.
With sensitive variations in pressure, Laura's pencil describes what she calls 'the ancient calligraphy' of rock strata along coastal Pembrokeshire.

Above **Virginia Hein,** *Climbing Rocks, Descanso Gardens Waterfall*, La Canada, California, USA, 2014.
I started drawing from the bottom, wanting to suggest mass and texture as I followed the climbing child, drawing rocks until I reached the child at the top, moving back downwards with the flowing water.

Below **Virginia Hein,** *Mystery Valley*, Monument Valley, Arizona, USA, 2011.
I enjoyed drawing this beautifully stark, rocky landscape with an almost continuous line. I was quite literally on a journey, in the back of a car!

Above **Caroline Johnson,** *Boats on the Shore*, Beer, Devon, 2008.
Caroline drew the harbour at Beer in Devon in the off-season – when it was very quiet – with a flowing pencil line, adding some textural strokes to suggest foliage on the cliffs.

Explore and observe

The artist Paul Klee said: 'A drawing is simply a line going for a walk.' I love that quote, because I often think of drawing as a journey. Just as there's more than one way to take a journey, there's more than one way to approach a drawing. One way is the 'unplanned journey': find an interesting spot from which to start your drawing, and start following your line like an interesting path to see where it takes you, without any particular destination in mind.

Tips to get you started

1 **Observe carefully** The most important thing you can do on your line journey is to observe carefully. Try looking at your subject more than you look at the drawing. When you are really observing, you respond to what you're seeing in a direct way, rather than drawing what you think or assume is there. You're not drawing just any tree that might be conjured up from memory, for instance; you are drawing a very specific tree at that moment in time.

2 **Feel the line** Let that tool, your pencil, pen or whatever, become a very natural extension of your hand. This takes practice! Try holding the tool in different ways; vary the pressure, vary the speed of your line. Notice how slow, steady pressure produces a line with a very different character from high-energy dashes and strokes. Strengthening this connection between your hand, the tool and the paper makes you a confident sketcher.

3 **Go for a ramble!** Start your journey with whatever strikes you as interesting in the scene. Let your tool move naturally from that point along a path. Practise slowing your pace, or speeding up, depending on the 'terrain' you're travelling. Enjoy all the twists and turns in the road, and let your line travel to a natural end before you start a new line.

4 **Follow the contours** Imagine that your hand is touching the surface that you are drawing – the edge of a tree trunk or the jagged crest of a hill. This really helps to strengthen the connection between not only the tool and your hand, but also your hand and your eye.

5 **Trust your eye** Keep observing. We so often want to fall back on memory, or what we think something looks like; this tends to produce a sameness to the shapes, silhouettes and lines we're drawing. Your eye may tell you something quite different from what you expect to see; practise trusting that.

Plan your journey

Another way to take a journey – and approach a drawing – is to have a plan. Just as you might use a map to plan a trip in advance, you can map out a drawing in much the same way with framing. When you approach a sketch like an unplanned journey, you start from a point and move outwards. When you start by drawing a frame, it sets apart that space from anything else, and in a sense you draw from the outside in.

Tips to get you started

1 **Draw a frame** When you frame a sketch by drawing a border first, you are creating a boundary – focusing your attention within that space and clearly defining the edges of your composition, like the view through a window. Framing helps you quickly design the elements of your sketch.

2 **Start small** A great compositional technique is making thumbnail sketches. Artists often make lots of small thumbnail sketches to try different compositions of the same subject, or very quickly catch the essence. Thumbnail sketches are small and super-quick; a small space naturally makes it easier for you visualise the whole, and to quickly simplify the most important elements you want to get across in your sketch.

3 **Design your sketch** Framing your sketch with a border is the first step in seeing the overall design. Like the viewfinder, it's another selection tool; you choose what to include and what to leave out of the window you've created. It becomes easier to see how each element, each line or shape you draw, affects

the whole composition – how a tall tree drawn in the middle of the sketch might appear to divide your drawing in half, for example.

4 **Find the rhythm** Rhythm in visual art is just as important as it is in music – a way to create a visual beat, which creates a sense of movement. When you attune yourself to seeing rhythms in your subject – like the pattern in a grove of trees, in flowing water or an arrangement of clouds – you begin to design your sketch around that rhythm. Your sketch then isn't just a collection of static objects; it's a dance that invites the eye in and moves it through your sketch.

5 **See the whole, and the parts** A great rule of thumb is to see and sketch the large shapes first, and then the parts – the smaller elements and details that, like puzzle pieces, make up the whole composition. That way, you decide what is important first and then add only the details that best support your visual story.

Left **Melanie Reim,** *One Hundred Views of Haystack Rock 1-6,* **Cannon Beach, Oregon, USA, 2014.**
Inspired by Hokusai's *One Hundred Views of Mt. Fuji,* Melanie made her own 100 views of Haystack Rock during a three-day visit.

Above **Virginia Hein,** *Rose Garden Thumbnails,* **La Canada, California, USA, 2016.**
In these little sketches I used line to describe contours and build mass, to explore patterns of light and shadow, trying different compositional formats.

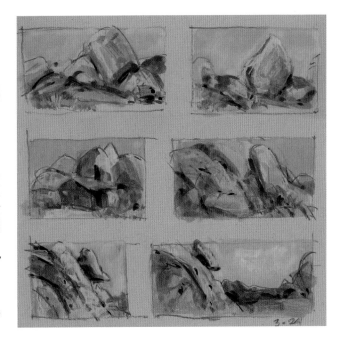

Right **Virginia Hein,** *Joshua Tree Thumbnails,* **Joshua Tree National Park, California, USA, 2016.**
I enjoy drawing rocks – endlessly fascinating forms and textures that seem to shift with the changing light.

Right **Virginia Hein, *Downhill*, Los Angeles, California, USA, 2015.**
In this passenger sketch riding towards downtown Los Angeles, I wanted to see if I could convey the distant skyline with loose, light pen strokes.

Below **Virginia Hein, *Depth Study, Descanso Gardens*, La Canada, California, USA, 2016.**
In this workshop demo sketch I wanted to show how rocks in the foreground appear large and have greater contrast compared to the figure and objects further back in the scene.

Above **Shari Blaukopf, *Farm Melt*, Ste.-Anne-de-Bellevue, Montreal, Canada, 2015.**
Notice how the trees in this lovely painting become less detailed further back in the scene, and the strong contrasts in the foreground compared to the background hills.

Below **Virginia Hein, *Glendale Freeway North*, Los Angeles, California, USA, 2015.**
For this passenger sketch heading towards the hills north of Los Angeles, I started with light colour washes, and then added ink line, leaving ink off the distant mountains to make them appear soft and hazy.

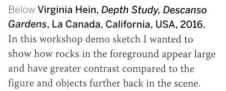

10-17

Create depth

There are a number of ways that we see and understand depth in a landscape, and interpret depth and dimension in a drawing. A great rule of thumb to keep in mind is this: whatever is closest to you appears larger, and what is further away appears smaller. We can show this with the placement and the relative size of things in a sketch, as well as with overlapping.

Tips to get you started

1 **Notice what's closest to you** To begin with, we'll refer to the two-dimensional surface on which you're sketching as the picture plane, and the ground in your landscape is literally the ground plane. You can basically separate what you see on the picture plane as foreground, middle ground and background. Notice how an object right in front of you in a scene, the foreground, not only appears larger than objects behind it, but typically is positioned low in the picture plane. This is how we see and instinctively understand depth and distance.

2 **Observe how forms overlap** I don't think there's any more effective way to show depth in a drawing than with overlapping shapes. No matter the size of an object, if it overlaps something else, we know it's in front. Notice how the combination of relative size, placement on the picture plane and overlapping shapes really work together to convincingly show depth in your sketch.

3 **Notice where you see contrast** In just about any weather, you'll notice the effects of atmosphere on a landscape. There's a great tendency to draw things as we think they are.

Clouds shading mountains in the distance, for example, may seem at first to be the darkest part of a landscape. However, if you look carefully, you'll notice that the contrast of the lightest light and the darkest dark generally appears right in front of you.

4 **Fade into the background** So, the furthest distance you can see in a landscape will be the most affected by atmosphere – an effect called aerial or atmospheric perspective. This is a key concept for any artist who wants to sketch landscapes with convincing depth! Notice how usually you will see less and less contrast in a scene the more distant it is, and how colour appears to fade as well.

5 **Lost and found** Notice where you see sharp edges in a landscape, and how atmosphere affects edges. Sharp, defined edges tend to draw the eye; notice how in nature you'll most often see the sharpest edges in the foreground. Lost edges are edges that appear to dissolve; notice how effective they can be in a sketch to show the effects of atmosphere on an object – and how it nudges it back in space.

Find your point of view

Seeing, understanding and interpreting depth in your
subject is all in your point of view! As seen in the previous topic, there
are lots of ways to convey depth, and perspective is just one aspect of
understanding and creating depth in your landscape drawing, as
well as conveying your attitude towards your subject.

Tips to get you started

1 **Where are you standing?** Linear perspective is the use of lines that converge on the horizon to show the position, size and shape of objects in relation to one another. While you might not expect to use linear perspective when drawing landscape subjects as often as you would when drawing architecture, for instance, some understanding of perspective is a useful tool to help you convey depth in a scene. Notice how the angle of your subject shifts as you move around – as you move your point of view.

2 **Look straight ahead** Now that you know how to find the horizon line in a scene by looking straight out ahead of you to find your eye level, notice how the lines of a road or path in front of you appear to converge at the horizon – this is a vanishing point. Your mind tells you that these lines are actually parallel, but your eye sees them converging, conveying a sense of distance. This is one-point perspective.

3 **Change your position** When sketching, you may see buildings or other objects in a landscape sitting at an angle to your point of view. Follow the angles of a house and notice how those angles recede in opposite directions; let your eye follow those lines to the horizon. This is two-point perspective.

4 **Watch the shadows** You know that shadows get longer as the sun lowers toward the horizon. Notice too how the angles of shadows appear to shift as you change position in relation to objects casting shadows.

5 **Notice the angles** Just as you may not actually see the horizon line in your landscape sketch if it's obscured by foliage or other objects, you might not see the vanishing points either. However, being able to visualise and understand these converging lines will help you quickly grasp scale and depth in a scene.

Above **Virginia Hein**, *Japanese Tea House, Descanso Gardens*, La Canada, California, USA, 2012.
It helps me to visualise the vanishing points of rooflines and other angles – especially when a building is partially hidden by foliage – before jumping into painting watercolour shapes.

Above left **Virginia Hein**, *December Drive Home*, Morongo Valley, California, USA, 2017.
One reason I enjoy passenger sketching on open roads is that I can easily see depth and perspective. The road creates an almost perfect one-point perspective vanishing towards the horizon line, while telephone poles diminish in size and distance apart as they extend for many miles.

Above **Caroline Johnson**, *The Path by the Wood*, Rawtenstall, Lancashire 2016.
Behind houses, an ancient pathway leads down the steep hill and into town. Fence posts and trees diminish in size as the path converges towards the horizon.

Right **Judith Alsop Miles**, *Ansignan Roman Aqueduct*, Ansignan, France, 2012.
Judith chose this striking point of view of the Roman aqueduct in spite of heat and lack of shade, working quickly with watercolour to capture the contrast of sun-baked stone and deep shadows in the arches.

A. Rule of thirds

✛ = Intersecting lines

B. Steelyard balance

Counterweight   Weight

Above **Virginia Hein, *Highway 10 Desert Drive*, Southern California, USA, 2011.**
Driving into the desert on a cloudy December morning, I was struck by the immensity of mountains and storm clouds next to the patch of light on the road.

Right **Virginia Hein, *Rule of Thirds: Rose Garden Gazebo*, Descanso Gardens, La Canada, California, USA, 2014.**
Here you see how the horizon line and the placement of the gazebo roughly correspond to intersections on the grid. Did I plan this? Not really! But, I do try to build compositions with shape relationships in mind.

C. Finished sketch

Left **Shari Blaukopf, *December Field*, Ste.-Anne-De-Bellevue, Montreal, Canada, 2015.**
There's a feeling of quiet serenity in this swiftly painted winter scene, with the two trees at left elegantly balancing the smaller tree at right. Notice how the stream moving towards the horizon seems to create a balance point.

Look for balance

The arrangement – the composition – of your subject is important; a strong composition draws the eye in and holds it. The challenge is to find balance in an interesting way. As humans, we seem to be drawn to symmetry, but asymmetrical balance in art can create a feeling of dynamic energy.

Tips to get you started

1 **Look at nature** There is certainly symmetry in nature – like the radial symmetry of flower petals – and elements that seem to repeat in a clear pattern: tree branches, veins in a leaf and so on. However, there are always interesting variations. Harmony in nature and in art is in the way a variety of elements work together.

2 **Consider the 'rule of thirds'** Again, there's a human tendency towards symmetry, but plunking your focal point in the middle of your sketch is usually the least interesting composition. A good way to offset the centre is a classic device used by artists, photographers, and cinematographers: the 'rule of thirds'. Simply put, you divide your page equally into thirds vertically and horizontally, and then place important elements along the intersections of the lines. This automatically pushes you out of the centre. That may sound a bit mechanical, but notice how an awareness of the rule of thirds helps you balance a composition in a more interesting way.

3 **Find contrast** When you create asymmetrical balance in a sketch, you have a play of contrasts. Contrast in a sketch draws the eye, and makes it interesting! A large object can balance with a grouping of smaller objects, for instance, like a mass of trees grouped together can balance with a few sparsely spaced trees.

4 **Balance with weight** Two early 20th century American landscape artists and teachers, Edgar Payne and Henry Rankin Poore, wrote about a number of ways to create balance in landscape composition – the most popular being 'steelyard balance'. A steelyard is basically a beam with a weight and a counterweight balanced on it. You can think of objects in your sketch composition as having weight, and a steelyard balance is a great way to create interesting asymmetry in your sketch, with a heavier element balancing a lighter element or grouping.

5 **It's all relative!** Composing a sketch is all about relationships. As you put each mark down on your page, see how it relates to what you have already done. You are making comparisons – one length of line next to another, the relative 'weight' of one shape as it balances with another. The same is true for values of light and dark as well as colour; it's the relationships between each shape, line and colour that give meaning to your sketch.

Leave something out

There is an art to knowing what to leave out of a sketch, and it's especially valuable with quick sketching. A key to this is understanding positive and negative space in art. We generally refer to subjects as positive space, and the area that surrounds the subjects as negative space. We can become so focused on trying to capture a subject that we disregard that surrounding space.

Tips to get you started

1 **Leave some space** The composer Claude Debussy said, 'Music is the silence between the notes.' In music, the silence, or the space between notes, is really what allows us to hear the music, and space between objects in a sketch works in much the same say. The negative space around your subject can eloquently draw your attention to it.

2 **See the whole page** With the choices you make of where to place subjects, you're composing the whole page. Notice how the space around your subject has a shape that interacts with the shape of the subject. Your eye does a kind of dance, seeing the subject – the positive space – and then seeing the negative shapes that surround the subject.

3 **Let your sketch breathe** Notice how leaving some space around your subject seems to give it some 'breathing room'. Negative space is sometimes called the 'white space', though it isn't necessarily empty or blank. In Japanese art, the concept of 'Ma' is very important. It means the space or pause between things – and like the silence between notes, in art it gives the eye a place to rest. There isn't quite

any English term for it, but negative space probably comes the closest. Practise allowing negative space in your sketch to play an important role.

4 **Say just what you need to say** A quick sketch frequently starts with the desire to capture something in the moment. There's often a temptation to just keep going and fill the page with detail that might not add much to your story. It takes some practice to get to the heart of what you want to say in your sketch, and leave it at that.

5 **Know when to stop** This can sometimes be the biggest challenge. Every artist at one time or another has surely said, 'I just overdid this'. I certainly have! The key is keeping an eye on the whole page. It takes a lot of practice to learn to artfully edit a sketch, and there will often be a lot of overworked sketches along the way. There's something to be learned from overdoing a sketch; it's how we begin to learn to eloquently leave something out.

Below right Shiho Nakaza, *Summer Colours*, Santa Monica, California, USA, 2015.
In this lovely sketch of a view looking down a tree-lined street, the negative space is as important as the colourful silhouette shapes of foliage, parked car and pedestrian.

Below Virginia Hein, Los Angeles *Arboretum View Across the Lake*, Arcadia, California, USA, 2015.
The Arboretum's Queen Anne Cottage is a landmark, but what intrigued me in this scene was the way it's almost engulfed by surrounding foliage. I felt the scene needed some white space to allow it to 'breathe'!

Above **Virginia Hein, *Highway 62 Meets Interstate 10*, Mojave Desert, California, USA, 2012.**
I usually draw both sides of the road with passenger sketching, but it seemed unnecessary to me here, especially with Mt. San Jacinto looming ahead on the right.

Allow breathing space

Negative shapes surround the subject

2

Strategies and techniques

So, let's jump in! In this chapter, we'll look at some ways to get you quickly sketching. I encourage you to be bold, and be ready to make 'mistakes' – lots of them! Think of what might look like a mistake to you as simply the result of an experiment. Quick sketching is a great antidote to perfectionism, a tendency that dogs many an artist. When you make a regular habit of quick sketching, you begin to lose the feeling of disappointment or failure if your sketch isn't exactly what you planned on: you know you can just turn the page and dive in again. This is the attitude of a quick sketch: welcome each 'mistake' and be open to every 'happy accident' as a door to new discoveries.

Left Looking up towards the road, I drew the large silhouette shapes of dry foliage in the foreground first, and dark shapes for the hills above to push them back in space.

Below **Suhita Shirodkar**, *Short Winter Days*, San Jose, California, USA, 2016.
Suhita had to work fast to capture the quickly fading light on a winter evening, using a very loose line to suggest all the bare branches of the trees in winter.

Above **Virginia Hein**, *Highway 395 North*, Eastern Sierras, California, USA.
My quick sketch 'training' has been years of sketching from the passenger seat on road trips – seeing how quickly I can put down impressions of the landscape rushing by. Of course, it helps when the terrain changes slowly!

Decide what it is in the scene that strikes you. Is it the 'big picture'...

...or the light, colour or structure?

Below **Uma Kelkar**, *On Way to Tahoe*, Sierra Nevada Mountains, California, USA, 2015.
Sketching from the highway, Uma used a reduced colour palette and the white of the paper to convey this snowy landscape, with the drama of jagged peaks and a winter sky.

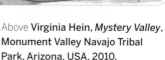

Above **Virginia Hein**, *Mystery Valley*, Monument Valley Navajo Tribal Park, Arizona, USA, 2010.
On a freezing New Year's Day, we had an unforgettable trip with a Navajo guide through Mystery Valley. She was used to stopping her car periodically so visitors could take quick photos. I'm not sure she'd seen anyone jump out to make quick sketches before!

Sketch on the go!

One of the great things about quick sketching is that it's something you can do on the fly. I always have at least one small sketchbook with me wherever I go, and never lack for subjects. Landscape subjects can be found in surprising places. I often do passenger sketching out the window on car trips and find little landscapes through café windows.

Tips to get you started

1 **Make a portable kit** You'll want to experiment with what works best for you – that's part of the fun of sketching. What you put in your kit will depend on the sketching situation; if you are on the go, keep it simple, at least to start with. Portability is the main factor here, as well as choosing your favourite sketching tools. A small sketchbook and a few pens and pencils are good to start with. Colour ink and markers are also quick and easy. Another consideration is whether you're standing or sitting; a small set of watercolours is great but not as easy to handle if standing, or in a crowd of people.

2 **Consider your time frame** Often quick sketching is born of necessity – you don't always have a lot of time to sketch for lots of reasons. That's when you want to consider what you can do in a short amount of time. It's amazing, though, once you acquire the sketching habit, how many opportunities actually arise.

3 **What do you want to capture?** In a quick sketch, you can't capture everything – but that's the fun and challenge of quick sketching: decide what it is in the scene that you're looking for. What is it that strikes you? Is it the 'big picture', an interesting area of the landscape or perhaps the light? Having an idea about what you're seeking helps you focus on that; let the rest wait for another day.

4 **Enjoy the process** The best way to jump fearlessly into quick landscape sketching is by focusing on the process of what you are doing, rather than the outcome. The great pleasure in quick landscape sketching is fully engaging in the moment – seeing and sensing the place you're in and exploring various materials and techniques.

5 **Experiment and play** While it's good to have an idea of what you want to capture in a sketch, you always want to be open to the unexpected. Be open to serendipity – those sudden occurrences or inspirations that can happen when you are sketching quickly, especially when sketching on location. Adopting the attitude of an experiment with your sketch helps relieve some of the pressure of an expected outcome, and helps you to be more spontaneous. Above all, take the attitude of play: sketch for the sheer enjoyment of it!

Simplify!

The artist Hans Hofmann said, 'The ability to simplify means to eliminate the unnecessary so that the necessary may speak.' When you look at nature, there is infinite complexity and detail. Before you can begin to simplify the landscape in your sketch, the challenge is to see and to choose what is essential in your landscape subject.

Tips to get you started

1 **Look for what is essential** Sketching a landscape on location is as much about seeing as it is about actual sketching. There is something very compelling and beautiful about a landscape sketch that expresses a scene in a clear and simple way – it catches the essence of the place and that moment in time. We recognise that essence because the artist sees it clearly. It's not just any mountain scene; it's that very specific mountain in that moment.

2 **See the silhouette** The most basic way to simplify a scene is to see it as a silhouette shape. Silhouette is a very powerful tool; we can instantly recognise people or objects in a familiar silhouette. Practise using the 'artist's squint' here, to 'push' the values of light and dark that you see to the darkest dark and lightest light. Practise sketching silhouette shapes working with one colour, in a medium that allows you to make bold shapes – soft pencil, watercolour, ink wash, marker and so on.

3 **Mass the shapes** Using the artist's squint again, notice how you can visually group objects together. A small grove of trees can become a single mass. Foliage can be very

challenging when you approach it as a multitude of leaves. Try instead to see where light and shadow create masses; this is key to simplifying your scene. Very importantly, though, be true to the shapes that you see, so that you maintain the character of the subject.

4 **Edit your subject** A great way to simplify your subject is to practise reframing your view. When confronted with a grand sweeping view, we often want to include the whole scope of what we see. Practise editing. Consider what you can leave out by reframing areas of your view (the viewfinder is very helpful here). Practise seeing a variety of possibilities within the scene, depending on where you focus.

5 **Capture, don't copy** What does it mean to 'capture a fleeting moment'? This is what an artist might hope to achieve in a quick landscape sketch – it suggests that you have somehow caught and held something of the essence of not just the scene, but the feeling and atmosphere of the place and time. It takes a lot of practice in seeing and *translating* what you see onto a page – letting go of any attempt to make a copy what you see.

Right **Virginia Hein**, *Ballona Wetlands*, **Los Angeles, California, USA, 2017.**
A quick lunchtime sketch at a nature reserve in the middle of Los Angeles. I wanted to simplify the scene by separating planes with silhouette shapes, and I used a very simple palette as well.

When confronted with a grand, sweeping view, consider what you can leave out and still retain the essence of the scene

Practise editing your scene by reframing areas of your view

You can focus on a few elements to make your sketch more powerful

Above **Tom Hoffmann**, *Wind-shaped Trees*, **Point Colville, Lopez Island, Washington, USA, 2016.**
Shapes are masterfully simplified in this landscape, but in a very specific way. Notice how the variety of hard and soft edges brings naturalness to the scene.

Above **Virginia Hein**, *Hidden Valley*, **Joshua Tree National Park, California, USA, 2016.**
In these little gouache studies I tried to keep the forms of rocks, foliage and sky simple, then added the detail of the tourists looking a bit like desert ants.

Left **Shari Blaukopf**, *Farm Field*, **Ste. Anne de Bellevue, Quebec, 2013.**
Shari painted this scene with just the essential shapes and a few colours. Note the soft edges in the background, crisper edges in the foreground. Catching a flock of birds in flight really adds energy and life!

Right *Virginia Hein, Ballona Wetlands Vertical View,* Los Angeles, California, USA, 2017. When I first looked at this scene, I noticed a strong pattern of diagonal lines, which prompted me to make a vertical sketch. I wanted to convey a feeling of flowing movement.

Below **Virginia Hein,** *Griffith Observatory from Barnsdall Park,* **Los Angeles, California, USA, 2011.** The 'star' of this sketch is clearly the Observatory (I've drawn it many times!); I wanted to stage it here with simple shapes in the landscape.

Diagonal lines create dynamic movement in your sketch...

...look for them in your landscape subject

A tree sketch in four stages, August 2014

Painting large wash shapes for foliage

Next, smaller areas of darker values in foliage

Then, painting in tree shadows, warmer yellows in foreground

Finally, more darks, colour and detail in foliage, trees and background – blues and violets for contrast

Work from large to small

You have only a few minutes to sketch. Start by considering what it is that made you want to sketch this particular scene. When you know what you want to include, work quickly to translate the big shapes onto your page, emphasising what's most important to you. Then develop the sketch with detail. Be selective; add details only if they support your initial impulse.

Tips to get you started

1 **See the large shapes first** Once you have a sense of what your subject is and what you want to include, the next step is to look at your landscape scene again. What are the largest shapes? Consider for a moment how you want to lay them out on your page.

2 **Block the actors in your story** For a stage play or on a film set, the director 'blocks' a scene by working out where actors should be positioned or move for dramatic effect – rather like choreographing a ballet. When you start a sketch, you can think of your page as that stage; you are looking at a landscape scene, but you are translating it into a sketch. In a sense you're directing the elements and actors of the scene. You can literally block in the shapes with whatever your medium is, or practise visualising them as you develop a sketch.

3 **Find a through-line** A through-line is a connecting theme or thread that ties a story together from start to finish. As you establish the large shapes, the most important elements of your sketch, look for ways you can add line, shape and colour that support your visual story.

You can certainly do this in a free and spontaneous way – building your sketch with pattern and repetition around a kind of visual through-line.

4 **Choose the most interesting details** Once you've established the essentials of your sketch, with the most important shapes and lines on your page, then it's a matter of choosing what you feel are the most important details – and the most interesting! Like the supporting players on a stage, consider how they work in relation to the main idea. With quick sketching these are very fast decisions; with a little practice they become almost an instinctive response to the scene and to your developing sketch.

5 **Suggest rather than explain** A quick landscape sketch is probably more like a poem than a novel. Not everything in your sketch has to be explained in detail, and quick sketching is a great way to learn this. Once you've decided what's essential in a scene, any additional details you might choose to include can be simply suggested.

Try different tools

Every tool you pick up has its own personality; even the way you handle it can affect the way you approach a sketch. Some tools are best for big, bold strokes, and lend themselves naturally to quick, spontaneous work. Others are better suited to fine, delicate work. Try working with brushes and other tools that allow you to be bold and expressive!

Tips to get you started

1 **Use a big brush** If you buy a small travel watercolour kit, it's likely it will come with a tiny brush. Or, perhaps you like the convenience of water brushes – understandable, there are certainly situations where they are ideal. However, I encourage you to pick up a really large brush and see what you can do with it, even if you're working on a small page. Every type of hair and shape of brush will give you very different results. Explore the way a large, round brush can give you thick, expressive strokes as well as detail, or the way a flat or angled brush can give you bold, flat strokes or defined edges, or how a mop gives you free, loose washes.

2 **Draw with broad strokes** You might use a hard lead pencil (the 'H's') to lightly map out a sketch, but for quick, expressive drawing, try a soft pencil (the 'B's'). The softer the pencil, the greater the range of light to dark you can achieve. The softest leads will give you rich, velvety blacks, and glide over the paper, while harder leads can dig into a paper surface if you push too hard. Soft pencils can be sharpened to give you a chisel tip to create varied strokes, or try a flat sketch or carpenter's pencil for wide and thin strokes with one tool.

3 **Loosen your hold** Changing the way you hold a pencil or a brush makes a big impact on your work; not only does it change the character of the marks you make, it can change the attitude you bring to the sketch. If your grip feels tight and controlled, see what happens if you loosen your hold, and change your hand position; you may feel out of control at first, but notice how your work quite literally loosens up. It's a lot like playing a musical instrument – the variations in touch create very different sounds!

4 **Test your tools** Every tool has its own personality and unique characteristics. Time spent practising, experimenting and getting to know those characteristics means that when you're out sketching in your landscape location, you are at ease with your materials.

5 **Try it a different way** When you're working with a new tool, you need to find out what it can do, or more importantly, what you can do with it. However, once you feel you've mastered that tool, it may be time to push yourself further; keep your work fresh by trying different tools and different approaches.

Left **Gail Wong,** *Arboretum Watercolour,* **Seattle, Washington, USA, 2015.**
Gail used a big brush and bold application of colour for this quick study.

Above **Virginia Hein,** *Moreton Bay Fig,* **South Pasadena, USA, 2014.**
This is an enormous tree and landmark in South Pasadena with great, spreading roots. I focused on the base here using a flat carpenter's pencil — great for quick sketching broad, flat strokes, or turn it sideways for sharp strokes.

Below *Virginia Hein, Joshua Tree Mountains,* **Joshua Tree National Park, California, USA, 2013.**
A quick impression of rocks and mountains with a calligraphy brush pen and water on absorbent paper.

Above **Tom Hoffmann,** *Elements,* **MacArdle Bay, Lopez Island, Washington, USA.**
Tom typically uses a 1½" slant-tipped wash brush. Here you can see he quickly established large, bold shapes with rich colour and strong contrast, with a combination of soft and hard edges.

Above **Pat Southern-Pearce, *Whalley Abbey Grounds*, Lancashire, 2010.** Pat often uses a palette knife in her elegant ink sketches, as she did here for the curving arcs of trees, along with a willow stick dipped in ink.

Left **Caroline Johnson, *Union Road, Rawtenstall*, Lancashire, 2016.** Caroline used coloured pencils and gouache to get a rich variety of line and textures in her sketch of a rural road bordered by stone walls.

Right **Don Low, *Dempsey Hill*, Singapore, 2013.** Don used a wide range of marks with ink and washes to convey the lush greenery and refurbished colonial buildings at this former nutmeg plantation.

Vary your marks

Mark-making is at the heart of drawing expressively. Every brushstroke, every pencil or pen line you make is a mark. We often recognise the style of an artist by their characteristic marks – they are as individual as handwriting. However, always making the same kind of marks for everything you do can get stale, so vary and experiment!

Tips to get you started

1 **Experiment with pressure** One of the most expressive tools you have is your own sense of touch. Whether using pencil, pen or brush, try varying the weight or pressure you use to create interesting variations in line weight. This is a great thing to practise for quick sketching – making strokes with varying pressure to strengthen that connection between your eye and your hand, and develop your confidence as a sketcher. Notice, too, how variations in line weight can quickly and effectively create the feeling of depth and weight in your subject.

2 **Express yourself!** Respond to your subject; you express feeling in every mark you make. Marks that slash and jab can communicate an angry, brooding storm; smooth, silky marks express something quite different. Calmness, excitement – every emotion influences the marks that give richness and character to your sketch.

3 **Be descriptive** In a quick landscape sketch you want to get to the point, to describe the sense of place and what inspires you about it with economy. Your marks can describe movement with variations in speed and direction. Build up marks to suggest texture, and notice how landscape elements like foliage, rocks and other surfaces are effectively conveyed with just some areas of texture, leaving space for the eye to fill in the rest.

4 **Bring some contrast** Contrast in your sketch draws your eye like a magnet. Consider all the ways you can bring contrast to a sketch with variations in your marks. Sharp-edged, bold marks can be like exclamation marks, demanding attention, especially as they contrast with soft, subtle areas of your sketch.

5 **Change the medium** It's easy to fall into a pattern of habitual marks by always using the same tool and the same materials – the tendency is to keep using them the same way. Explore the characteristic marks of every medium. Fountain pens, bamboo and dip pens can create expressive and sometimes unpredictable marks, so different from a pen with precise line width. Keep experimenting; there is real excitement in a sketch that teeters on the brink of control!

Work small

You would expect that by working on a small scale, you'd be more likely to finish a sketch quickly. But there are many good reasons to work small. Working on a small page, especially in a sketchbook, gives you a lot of freedom; you may be more likely to experiment, to try something you've never done before without a big investment of time and materials.

Tips to get you started

1 **Find the right size** British artist Henry Moore said, 'There is a right physical size for every idea.' While working small is great for sketchbook sketching and quick sketching in general, it's also perfect when you just want to express a simple idea of your landscape. Often artists do a small sketch with the intention of creating it in a larger format later, where there's a temptation to elaborate past the point of the impact you had in the original sketch. There is something about filling a small page with a large idea; it can have tremendous impact.

2 **Draw super-quick thumbnails** Personally, I love making thumbnail sketches. I find it a great way to get a composition down as quickly as possible – to cut to the chase, so to speak. Just as the name implies, a thumbnail sketch is very small – perhaps postage stamp-size to business card-size; any larger and there's a great temptation to over-elaborate. You can say everything you need to in a little thumbnail in two minutes! If you're making multiple thumbnails on a page, be sure to leave some space around each little image, whether or not you draw a frame. It's important to contain that idea, that little composition, so that it stands apart clearly.

3 **Play with scale** Try changing up the scale of your subject with different thumbnail studies to see what works. When you look at your landscape subject, use your artist's squint to observe the large shapes. What if you cropped everything except that which is most interesting to you?

4 **Work from one to the next** Making multiple small sketches on a page is a great way to quickly explore a variety of ways to compose your subject. Don't plan these in advance; instead let each sketch lead you to the next one.

5 **Paint a sketch** Try painting big and bold with a big brush, but on a small page. This is a great way to see how large areas of colour interact with each other. Try a broad, flat brush, which makes it harder get lost in detail. You may find that your sketch looks quite abstract with this approach, but all the better to focus on the design. Keep it simple – start with the biggest brush, then use smaller brushes just to add essential details.

Right **Virginia Hein, *Thumbnails from the Front Porch*, Twentynine Palms, California, USA, 2015.**
I made these tiny thumbnails on the porch of an old adobe house on the outskirts of a Mojave Desert town, quickly layering pencil, watercolour and gouache.

Below **Uma Kelkar, *Imagine 2*, near Manchester, 2016.**
Uma made this atmospheric little watercolour sketch recalling scenes from the train – rolling hills, sunlight in the middle ground, and the feeling of loneliness of the old stone cottages.

Bottom **Shiho Nakaza, *Lunchtime: Foggy Day*, Playa Vista, Los Angeles, California, USA, 2017.**
This is one of a series of small sketches Shiho made from a patio view at work during lunchtime. Here she captures the feeling of dense atmosphere.

Above **John Banh, *Snow-Capped Mountains*, Griffith Park, Los Angeles, California, USA, 2017.**
This little gem was painted in gouache at an urban park, looking unusually green due to recent rain showers. The water brush shows the scale.

Viewfinder

Right **Virginia Hein,** *Tea House Gouache Study,* Descanso Gardens, La Canada, USA, 2016.
Here I'm using half of my viewfinder to compare the roof angle to the right angle corner. While it helps to understand some basic perspective when sketching, this is a great way to learn to trust your eye.

Below **Virginia Hein,** *Japanese Garden Trees,* Descanso Gardens, La Canada, USA, 2015.
Another way I use my pencil 'gauge' is to compare angles and curves with a straight vertical or horizontal. There's often a tendency to straighten out the curving posture of a tree, or draw branches at right angles; this helps in seeing the graceful asymmetry of natural forms.

Use the viewfinder to compare angles

Here I'm using my pencil tip to gauge the width of a tree trunk. I can then use that width to quickly compare to the length of the trunk, the widths of branches or the proportions of other trees.

Use your pencil to compare angles and curves

Again, I'm measuring the length of a palm tree to compare with the overall width of the palm fronds. This helps me quickly get a sense of relative proportions.

Measure with your eye

It's worthwhile visualising the entire composition of your sketch – a great strategy regardless of the amount of time you have. Start by visualising the 'big picture' on your page. Gauge proportions with your eye, or with the aid of a handy tool, like your pencil. Trust your eye; don't draw what you expect to see.

Tips to get you started

1 **Visualise the whole picture** Take a moment to envision your landscape sketch on the page, even before you make a single mark. This accustoms you to seeing your scene in the format of the page, with all the elements you want in it. With practice, you begin to see the scene playing out before you, along with areas of negative space. Clearly, the process of sketching involves lots of decisions along the way – what to include and what to leave out – but that practise in seeing the landscape translated to your page is tremendously helpful.

2 **Use your pencil** I grew up seeing cartoons in which an artist would start a picture by sticking out his thumb in front of his subject, which always seemed so silly to me. Many years later, I discovered what that was about: an easy way to measure! Your pencil or pen is a very effective way to gauge proportions. Hold your pencil out straight in front of you at arm's length to gauge the length of a subject – a tree trunk, fence post and so on. That becomes a unit of measure as you turn your hand vertically or horizontally. For example, a fence width might be double the length of one post.

3 **Find the angles** Another way to use your pencil 'gauge' is to hold it vertically or horizontally to compare angles. If you're looking at a leaning tree, or the rooftop of a building, you can compare the degree of angle with your pencil. Your viewfinder, the cardboard 'L' described in Chapter 1, can do much the same thing.

4 **Focus on relationships** Every line or shape you draw works in relation to the rest of your sketch. Observe how those shapes and lines relate to one another on the page. With practice, you'll see how each element you add relates to the rest of the picture while you are sketching – how each part affects the rest. This goes back to the idea of a director blocking the actors on a stage; it's all about the relationships between those actors. 'Direct' your sketch!

5 **Follow your eye** Ultimately, you want to trust the process and follow your own eye. You bring your own point of view to the sketch with your own interpretation. You may choose to intentionally emphasise something with exaggeration or to distort for effect. Let that override concerns about exact measurements. Allow the picture to lead you as it develops.

Choose your surface

So far we've referred mainly to sketchbooks. However, there's no end of supports and surfaces you can use to sketch on, including a wide variety of papers, each with their own unique characteristics to add a different flavour to your sketch. What you choose as a sketching support or surface has to do with the effect you're after.

Tips to get you started

1 **What's your media?** Deciding on a surface begins with your media. For pencils, a paper with a smooth surface usually works best – notice how the finish affects the line quality. Every media will work differently on different types of supports. A 'hard-sized', smooth paper works great for ink, while a paper which has a 'tooth' allows dry media like graphite, coloured pencil, pastel and crayon to grab the surface. With watercolour you want to consider absorbency and how much detail you want.

2 **Supports and surfaces** Anything that allows you to make a mark on it can be a support for your sketch, so it's a matter of deciding on the type of surface you want. Drawing papers can have a plate or smooth finish, ideal for ink and drawings with detail, or a velvety, vellum finish, ideal for dry media. Vellum-finish papers are often used with mixed-media, since they can usually take a light watercolour wash. Consider the weight of the paper as well; for wet media, to avoid buckling choose a paper that's a minimum of 120 to 150 gsm.

3 **Rough or smooth?** Watercolour paper is available in three different surfaces. Hot press is smooth, ideal for detailed painting and also

works well with dry media or ink; the downside is that it's not as forgiving with wet washes. Cold press paper has a subtle texture and is more absorbent than hot press paper. Rough watercolour paper has the most texture and absorbency, so it's most often used for wet into wet techniques and textural effects. The best watercolour papers are made of 100% cotton rag – more durable than wood pulp paper.

4 **Choose a sketchbook** You can find sketchbooks with all kinds of paper and quality, including watercolour sketchbooks with heavier, cold press paper, and tinted papers. My advice is to start with a good quality sketchbook or sketchpad, but not so expensive that you're afraid to ruin it with a 'bad' sketch!

5 **Other kinds of supports** Watercolour blocks, pads and single sheets come in different weights and qualities. A block keeps the paper stretched as you paint; once the painting is dry, you remove the sheet by sliding a palette knife underneath. Blocks are convenient for working on location, although the disadvantage is that you can only use one sheet at a time. Most sketching is done on paper, but consider artist's sandpaper, hardboard, mat board or cardboard.

Rough paper is great for dry-brush texture

Below **Tom Hoffmann**, *Dawn, South End*, Lopez Island, Washington, USA, 2015.
In this atmospheric painting, Tom suggests textures of trees and foliage.

Above **Kris Wiltse**, *Morning Sunlight*, Whidbey Island, Washington, USA, 2011.
Kris painted this lovely watercolour sketch with wet watercolour washes, allowing some colours to softly bleed.

Cold press paper shows watercolour granulation

Below **Virginia Hein**, *Los Angeles Hillside, November*, Los Angeles, California, USA, 2009.
I used soft pencils (2B and 6B) on a hot press watercolour paper, as I wanted strokes and detail to be clear.

Hot press paper is good for pencil detail

Left **Virginia Hein,** *Descanso Gardens Trees on Grey Paper*, **La Canada, California, USA, 2015.**
Here I experimented with starting from a mid-value grey paper, drawing darks with a carpenter's pencil and adding the light with white china marker.

Below **Virginia Hein,** *Arboretum Eucalyptus*, **Arcadia, California, USA, 2015.**
I made a quick ink sketch of this tree, and then added a grey wash to catch the late afternoon light and shadow.

Right **Virginia Hein,** *Eucalyptus Tree*, **Loyola Marymount University, Los Angeles, California, USA, 2017.**
A soft, terracotta colour pencil allowed me to quickly build shadows and texture in the tree and surroundings, using the point and side of the pencil.

Below **Gabriel Campanario,** *Yaquina Lighthouse*, **Newport, USA, 2013.**
Gabi challenged himself to find a variety of texture and patterns using hatching and cross-hatching to describe this rocky coastal landscape.

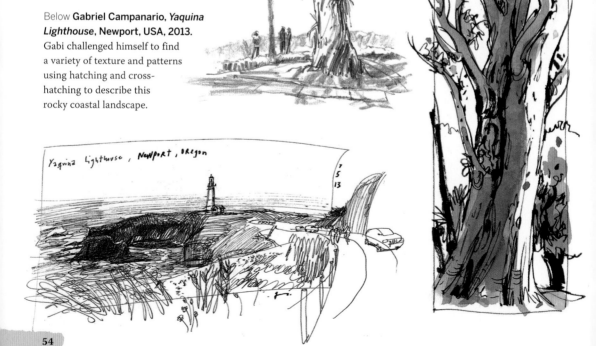

Sketch in monochrome

Monochrome isn't just black and white; it can be varying tones of any colour from light to dark. When working in monochrome, you are focused on form and translating the scene quickly into values, rather than colour. Learning to see the value range within a colour is key to working successfully with colour. In addition, a monochromatic sketch can be beautiful in its own right.

Tips to get you started

1 **Sketch with a pencil** Pencil is great for tonal drawing, and a soft pencil will give you a wide range of values. With tonal drawing, you are focused on differentiating objects with value shifts rather than outlines. We see shapes primarily because of tonal differences. With fast landscape sketching, you can quickly rough out a sketch with tones, following patterns of light and dark. You can swiftly build tonal contrast with a soft pencil, varying soft and hard edges.

2 **Draw with a pen** You can develop a lovely range of textures and tones just with pen – grouping marks, using line and texture to suggest forms, and hatching (a classic technique to create tone and shading with more or less parallel lines). For quick sketching, ink line and texture is most effective contrasted with areas of negative space or added tonal washes.

3 **Add some washes** Start with ink or pencil line, and then build tone with layers of diluted ink or watercolour washes – building tones with increasing density of pigment. For quick landscape sketching, you want to limit the passes, to save time and not 'muddy' the layers. It's easier to learn basic watercolour painting techniques in monochrome, such as how much water to use. A simple line drawing may only need a few areas of tonal wash to add depth and interest.

4 **Build the values** Tonal sketching can be very exciting with a full range of values. Try 'pushing' the landscape's values to create more drama and make a more dynamic sketch. There's a tendency on the part of beginner sketchers to hold back on value contrast. Developing a sensitivity to values and shifts of dark and light is valuable whether you work in monochrome or full colour.

5 **Try dark to light** Try starting with dark grey or even black paper. It's fascinating and challenging to reverse the usual process of building from light to dark – starting with a mid-tone and building the darks as well as the light. It makes you very conscious of adding light, and can create a wonderful, moody effect.

Paint with a limited palette

Why a limited palette? The obvious benefits are that a few colours are more portable and less expensive. More importantly, by using just a few colours, your colour sketch will likely be more harmonious. For now we'll focus on watercolour, although a limited palette works well with a variety of colour media, especially with limited time. Make a chart of the colours in your palette; become familiar enough with it to make quick colour decisions.

Tips to get you started

1 Do more with less For quick landscape sketching, you don't need a lot of colours – four, five or six well-chosen mixing colours can give you rich, harmonious colour combinations. You may want to change your palette depending on your sketching location. When I sketch in the Mojave Desert, I use earth colours much more than I do at home. I don't find any need for black in my palette, since I can mix rich neutrals with a combination like blue and burnt sienna.

2 Notice 'colour temperature' We think of colours as having a temperature – warm or cool. Looking at the colour wheel, the reds and yellows are 'warm', blues and violets appear more 'cool'. However, there are cool reds (those veering towards blue) and warm reds, warm blues (veering towards red) and cool blues. You may see a mix of warm and cool in a landscape scene, but one or the other predominates – often blues in the morning, warmer tones later.

3 Choose complements A great way to experiment with warm and cool is to work with any two complementaries (opposites) on the colour wheel, since one will tend to be warmer and one cooler. It's helpful to try working with complementaries after you have explored a range of values in monochrome. Notice what happens when you work with pure, saturated hues of those colours, and what happens as you mix greater or lesser amounts of each colour.

4 Try a triad A triad is a combination of three colours equally spaced on the colour wheel. For example, the primary colours of red, blue and yellow are a triad. Try variations on this mix to see what a full range of colours you can achieve. Let one colour predominate, otherwise the three hues will battle for dominance.

5 Contrast and harmony With a few colours in your palette, and some practice with mixing, you will see ways to create contrast where you want it – not only contrast of light and dark, but of colour hues. Developing most of the sketch with a few colours to create harmony, and then adding a few pops of contrasting colour here and there is dynamic! Harmony may be created with analogous colours (hues adjacent on the colour wheel), or by mixing colours across the colour wheel to make them less saturated.

Right **Tom Hoffmann, *Lopez Island*, South End, Washington, USA, 2013.**
Blue-violets dominate the colour palette here and clearly register the temperature in this scene, and the soft, pale complementary orange in the sky is a lovely counterpoint.

Below **Shiho Nakaza, *Lunchtime: Cloudy Day*, Playa Vista, Los Angeles, California, USA, 2017.**
In this little watercolour sketch, Shiho effectively used a limited palette of blues, violets and a pale gold in her study of winter clouds.

Create harmony by mixing with a limited palette

Below **Marion Rivolier, *The Sculpture in the Jardin des Tuileries*, Paris, France, 2015.**
Late October trees with yellow, orange, red and purple foliage created a dramatic background for the sculpture by Smiljan Rajic and Marcela Correa. Marion began with large brushstrokes, then added a few details.

A landscape scene will have cool and warm tones; notice if one is more dominant in the scene than the other and let it lead your sketch

Left **Shari Blaukopf,**
Canola, **Alexandria,**
Ontario, Canada, 2015.
The delicate calligraphy of
Shari's ink line beautifully
complements the watercolour
washes, which was applied in
broad strokes.

Below **Virginia Hein,** *Rose Garden*
Ink and Wash, **Descanso Gardens,**
La Canada, California, USA, 2016.
I made this quick sketch in ink,
keeping in mind where I wanted to
then paint areas of wash and leave
open areas of negative space.

Above **Pat Southern-Pearce,**
The Yorkshire Dales, **2010.**
Pat pushed this sketch of dry
stone walls zigzagging the
landscape towards elegant
abstraction using brilliant
coloured inks, applied with
pen, brush and palette knife.

Line and colour

Many location sketchers favor the combination of ink and colour, especially waterproof ink with watercolour washes. This is a quick and very portable combination, and a quick and easy way to get line, shape and colour into your landscape sketch.

Tips to get you started

1 **Start with expressive line** The usual method is to start with a line drawing. Consider where you want line definition in your sketch. How much line do you need? You are working with two complementary media here; ink is ideal for expressive line, while colour can be applied in broad strokes.

2 **Leave areas open** As you make an ink drawing, think about where you can leave some open areas, some passages in your sketch that will be carried by colour washes. Where do you want to leave the white of the paper? A unique characteristic of watercolour is that light is conveyed by the white of the paper. Leaving areas of white in your sketch creates sparkle and freshness.

3 **What do you want to emphasise?** Especially with quick sketching, you may want to do a line drawing and only add a few areas of colour for emphasis. Just notice how colour immediately draws the eye.

4 **Let line and colour dance!** When you're working with ink and watercolour washes, let the character of each shine. The media of ink line and colour shape are much more exciting when they can play complementary roles in your sketch. Avoid the 'colouring book' technique of simply filling in your lines. Let your colour overlap the line, bleed a little, and leave spaces of white to let the line and colour breathe.

5 **Experiment with different inks** Notice the differences in line quality you can get with a fibre tip or rollerball pen compared to a brush pen, a fountain pen or calligraphy pen. A dip pen or bamboo pen can give you exciting line variations. But you're not limited to black ink; there are many colour ink pens that are fairly waterproof, and a colour ink line will soften the effect of the line in your sketch. Water-soluble inks are another option to work with line and wash and add some unpredictability! It's easy to overdo it – just a bit of water will release a tint from the line. It takes a little practice with a deft hand to use just enough water and brush away from the line in one direction, allowing some crispness of the line to remain.

Focus on watercolour

With quick landscape sketching, painting directly with watercolour shapes is a wonderful way to push yourself towards simple, bold compositions. It is sometimes said that watercolour is an art of silhouette, and you can communicate a lot with attention to edges. Contrast crisp edges with some areas of wet washes. Let this way of working push you towards abstraction. Use bold shapes to convey the feeling of the landscape.

Tips to get you started

1 **Try the 'wet into wet' technique** For quick landscape sketching you may not have time to start with an entire wet page. However, you can choose areas where you want graded or blended washes. A wash is a semi-transparent layer of colour usually applied with a broad brush. You can brush colour for a sky on to a pre-moistened area of your sketch and it will bleed into the wet area only. This is a great way to convey atmosphere in your sketch – clouds, water, the effects of weather on the landscape.

2 **Create a few layers** Generally, we work from light to dark, starting with the most diluted, light colours. Subsequent layers are usually darker and heavier in consistency. With quick sketching, you probably won't add more than a layer or two; let them blend! Much of the beauty of watercolour is its luminosity, so allow some white of the paper to shine through. While the brightest light comes from reserving the white of the paper, I carry some opaque white with me to sometimes add a bit of white back in!

3 **Mix some natural greens** In many landscapes, you'll see a range of greens. In a tropical climate, the greens can be quite vivid, while in a desert or a northern winter latitude the greens may be very subtle. To create a rich range of greens on your palette, try a mix of yellow and blue. Experiment with a warm blue like cobalt or ultramarine with yellows, or a cool blue like cerulean or phthalo for more vivid greens.

4 **Try mixing on the paper** When you allow your colours to mix on the paper instead of your palette, you're exploiting one of the most joyous characteristics of watercolour. While your first colour wash is still wet, drop or lightly brush some pigment onto the wet surface, allowing the colour to blend freely. You'll see a much more brilliant mix with unexpected variations than you would with a pre-mixed colour. Add more pigment than water. Avoid 'scrubbing' your brush, as that tends to pick up pigment.

5 **Watercolour and weather** When you're out sketching landscapes with wind and weather it can be exciting – and unpredictable! Humid tropical weather can make watercolour a bit sticky and slow to dry, and of course desert dryness and heat will do just the opposite. A small spray bottle with water is helpful to lightly spray your palette in hot weather.

Left **Suhita Shirodkar, *Clouds Over Dogpatch*, San Francisco, California, USA, 2016.**
Suhita painted the billowing clouds wet into wet, transforming this urban landscape. Some architectural details were added as the paint was drying.

Wet into wet

Here I'm painting wet into wet – first a wash of warm yellow (Hansa medium).

At top I've dropped in ultramarine blue, to create subtle greens, typical of greens I see in Southern California's semi-desert, or greens that are affected by atmospheric colour.

I added phthalo blue at bottom; as you see, it's super-saturated and makes a brilliant green. A little of this goes a long way!

Below **Virginia Hein, *Last Light in an Urban Valley*, Los Angeles, California, USA, 2009.**
I painted this on a summer evening, just as foliage became a dark silhouette against the sky. I treated the foliage as one large shape, so I could focus on the sky colours. I dropped violet into damp pink cloud shapes as the light began to fade.

Below Virginia Hein, *The Rose Garden*, Descanso Gardens, La Canada, California, USA, 2011.
I started with the large silhouette shapes of trees and sky, leaving the shape of the gazebo mostly white. I added splotches of colour in the foreground for the flowers and finished with pencil line for detail.

Right Virginia Hein, *Twentynine Palms Sketch*, Mojave Desert, California, USA, 2014.
This is a view I've painted often; on a cloudy December afternoon I wanted to approach it differently. I painted large areas of wash, letting the colours bleed, and then drew into the damp paint with soft pencil.

Below Suhita Shirodkar, *Tuscan Countryside, Storm Approaching*, Italy, 2016.
Watercolour was applied with flowing, loose strokes in this delightful sketch as a storm approached, and Suhita had to run for shelter! Pencil line defines a few details in the landscape and building.

Start with colour

Another technique is to reverse the usual process of sketching with line and colour – start with the colour first. This is great to try if you have a hard time not 'filling in the lines' with your sketches. Start with some bold colour shapes and be loose and free with them. Try different media for adding some line into the sketch. You may discover that you don't need as much line as you thought.

Tips to get you started

1 **Think in shape** Take a little time to study your landscape. Where do you see the large shapes and areas of colour? I find it interesting that when you approach the sketch with a large brush in hand, rather than a fine point drawing tool, you think differently; that large, shape-making tool helps you actually think in shape. Be free and bold with your paint application, but also keep an eye on the silhouette shapes you're creating.

2 **Keep it fresh** Keep it fresh by laying down some colour washes, and letting them be! Don't try to work back into those shapes; perhaps add a drop more pigment to mix on the page. Give some thought as you paint to where you'll leave some white space, and where you'll add some line.

3 **Choose your line** Try some different tools and techniques for adding line – 'less is more' definitely applies here. You can get some exciting effects by drawing with a water-soluble colour pencil directly into a wet wash. Ink, of course, will bleed, and other dry media will have different effects – water-soluble crayon, pastels and so on. You may want to wait until your sketch is dry, and then might discover that you don't need much line, if any.

4 **Decide 'who's boss'** Here is yet another 'dance': let one or the other element predominate. Perhaps it's a colour sketch with just a bit of line definition. Or, a few colour splotches are scattered on the page with a more detailed line drawing on top. Allow the elements to interact with each other in an interesting and edited way – just enough!

5 **Leave some sparks** Areas of pure colour with minimal line allow the imagination of the viewer to fill in more of the story. Also notice how sparks of the white of the paper really enliven a sketch and keep it fresh.

Splash and splatter

Have some fun with watercolour! There are myriad ways of creating texture and other exciting effects in your quick landscape sketch. Be open to some unexpected results! Try some different techniques to suggest some of the beautiful textures that are found in nature – this will add a lot of interest to your quick sketch.

Tips to get you started

1 **Create texture** There are lots of ways to quickly add textures in your landscape sketch using watercolour. Try snapping the bristles of your paintbrush to create a spatter texture – great for textures of earth and rock, and fun too. The results are a little random, but that's part of what adds to a feeling of spontaneity. A rough watercolour paper is ideal for textures made with a dry brush. A natural sea sponge dipped in your paint will give you interesting textures for clouds, rocks and so forth. I don't usually carry salt on location, but sprinkling salt into a wet wash will absorb some water and leave an interesting pattern.

2 **Be bold** Some of these techniques for creating texture can produce random-looking results, but don't let that scare you! Part of the joy of working on location, out in a natural setting, is being open to unexpected results – and it adds to the spontaneity of your work.

3 **Let it be** Don't worry about 'mistakes' as you create a quick landscape sketch. I don't recommend using an eraser (except for cleaning up the occasional smudge), or doing a lot of paint 'lifting' when you're quick sketching

on location, for several reasons. It's easy to overwork a sketch, and just 'letting it be' is usually the best course. Erasing lines in your sketch tends to make you second-guess yourself, and slows you down. Let all the 'mistakes' be part of the process; believe it or not, that can add excitement to your sketch!

4 **Work with drips and bleeds** Things happen when you're out in nature sketching! It can start to rain, and suddenly you have a fine mist in your painting or drips you didn't plan on. Or, in a burst of enthusiasm (or a high wind!), you dribble and drip some paint. Try to work with it; let it be part of the experience and part of your sketch! Sometimes those unexpected things can add tremendously to the 'atmosphere' of your painting.

5 **Be in the moment** I can't emphasise enough that if you enjoy the process of sketching and being out in a natural environment, it will absolutely show in your sketch! I like quick sketching especially because it can sidestep any tendency towards deliberating and doubt. You are in the moment!

Left **Liz Steel, *After the Storm*, Flynn's Beach, Port Macquarie, New South Wales, Australia, 2013.**
After a big storm, the ocean was filled with dirty foam, so Liz focused on the contrast of pale ocean foreground and the dark silhouettes of cliffs and trees. Splatters here add to the feeling of splashing surf!

Right **Laura Murphy Frankstone, *On a Boat in December, Moving Ever Northward*, Arctic Norway, 2009.**
Sketched on the last day of an Arctic trip in watercolour and Pentel pocket brush pen, Laura felt she had finally 'devised a shorthand that could express the crystalline cold and stark beauty of that world'. Some water spray adds to the icy texture!

Below **Virginia Hein, *Passenger Sketch with Pink Mountains*, Los Angeles, USA, 2016.**
I was trying out a new pen with surprising results – I didn't expect it to bleed that bright fuchsia wash! I went with it, adding some splashes and splatters of gold and yellow.

As you make your quick line sketch, take a note of the colour, tone and feeling of the scene

Right Virginia Hein, *Eucalpytus*, **Black and White and Colour, Los Angeles, USA, 2017.**
During a lunch hour, I had just enough time to visit this old eucalyptus and make a quick ink sketch. I later returned when I had a bit more time to add colour. Returning to a sketch later on can be tricky – the weather or your own mood may be quite different!

Make notes so you can continue working on your sketch when you have more time

Below Pat Southern-Pearce, *Brinham Rocks*, **W. Yorkshire, 2014.**
With rain threatening, Pat had to sketch quickly 'with fierce focus, making every line count!' Her beautiful calligraphy describing the process was added later, and completes the scene.

Later you can add a full range of values. You may decide to add more line definition or a final layer to the sketch.

Leave something for later

Landscape sketching is often quick purely because of limited time. Perhaps you're with family or a group of non-sketchers, you're on a lunch hour, or simply don't have a lot of time! One good strategy is to sketch what you can on location, with the thought of what you can add later.

Tips to get you started

1 **Draw line for now** Perhaps you have time just for a quick line drawing. Nevertheless, as you observe and sketch, you can form an impression of the colour, the feeling and the tone of the landscape, with a thought to adding colour later A bit of colour can add some mood, or direct the viewer's attention to something. However, you may find as you look at your sketch later that it doesn't need much colour, or that maybe the line is enough.

2 **Colour notes** Many sketchers find it helpful to make notes about the colour, or about the mood of the location. This can be a great aid to your memory, and actually can add an interesting element of narrative to your sketch.

3 **Add colour later** A few little colour 'swatches' on your sketch can help aid your memory. Often when you add colour to a sketch later on, it has a very different feel to it than colour added on location. I find it challenging to reproduce observed light, to convey a feeling of natural light. Adding a note about light source can help.

4 **Add another layer** Sometimes you look at a sketch later and feel it needs something. I have on occasion found I can get line and colour into a quick landscape sketch, but didn't have time to develop a full range of values, for instance. I might later add a final layer to the sketch – or add a bit more line definition. Sometimes that works and gives the sketch the punch it needs. But sometimes it falls into the category of overworking, and I wind up wishing I'd left well enough alone!

5 **Do what works for you** Your eye doesn't see the same way a camera does – why should it? Not only do you interpret what you see and bring impressions and feelings about the landscape that are absent from the camera, but the camera simply 'sees' light, values and colour differently. If you take a picture of a scene with the thought of using it to finish a sketch later, it's tempting to go back and rework your sketch to 'match' the photo. That does work for some artists. Most importantly, you should do what works for you.

Focus on landscape elements

L et's get down to the specifics of quick landscape sketching – all the interesting elements that make up a landscape, as well as the character of different landscapes and how you might approach them. We'll also look at the fascinating effects of weather and atmosphere – how they can change a landscape dramatically in an instant and greatly affect the mood. And we'll look at the variety of natural features of the Earth's surface – such as mountains and canyons – that create the specific terrain of a landscape.

Left I added a wash to the foreground, distant mountains and the long connecting strip of road to help convey the sense of distance here.

Right **Simo Capecchi, *Fagus*, Abruzzo, Italy, 2011.**
'Fagus' is Latin for beech – Simo uses a lively variety of textures to convey the foliage. She reports the words of a passerby: 'Look at that tree, it's so beautiful it should be painted... oh, that lady IS drawing it!'

Left **Shari Blaukopf, *December*, Beaconsfield, Quebec, 2013.**
In this elegantly simple sketch, Shari shows the graceful variations of tree shapes in a winter landscape, as well as the natural variation of intervals between trees.

Right **Melanie Reim, *Gurney's Inn Winter Beach*, Montauk, New York, USA, 2015.**
With a rich variety of materials and marks, Melanie conveys the feeling of winter weather at this northeast coast beach, with the hardy grasses blowing in the wind.

No two the same

We all grow up learning that no two snowflakes are the same – and
it's true for everything else in nature. There is an abundance of patterns in
nature and elements that seem to repeat – petals on a flower, veins in a leaf,
branching of trees – but just like snowflakes, no two are really alike.

Tips to get you started

1 **See natural variation** Notice how even when trees have been planted equidistantly apart, they grow in their own individual ways. Branch patterns will vary, very rarely appearing symmetrical. In a wild landscape, you'll see tremendous variations in how things grow and develop. Whether you are observing elements close up – such as variations in leaves, flowers or rocks – or standing back to observe how water flows or how foliage branches in various directions, keep observing the variations.

2 **Vary the patterns** Patterns are everywhere in nature. Tree growth is marked by rings, segments of branches follow patterns. We can see distinct spiralling patterns in flowers, seed pods and pinecones. Avoid the tendency to generalise those patterns; while the pattern is distinct and recognisable, it's important to see how it changes and varies, and equally important to include those variations in sketches. Don't let your indication of pattern become mechanical, as might be the case in manmade objects.

3 **Notice the intervals** Intervals are the spaces or pauses between things, and they are very important in nature as well as in your sketch.

In a grove or forest, the spaces between trees might seem the same, but if you look closely there are always variations. You'll capture a convincing feeling of nature if you vary the intervals in your sketch.

4 **Create variety** Your sketch will be more exciting when it has a dynamic range. Vary the elements; consider using one medium to describe silhouette shapes and another to suggest detail. Suggestion is important here – you don't have to cover your page with detail; in fact it's more effective to leave areas that allow the viewer to fill in more of the pattern.

5 **Play with textures** One of the most exciting and interesting things about being out in a natural landscape is seeing the range and richness of textures. Of course, with quick sketching, you won't have time to render every texture. Finding ways to suggest texture is part of the fun of quick sketching. The roughness of some tree barks, the surface of rocks, the delicacy of grasses or flowers – these can be suggested with a range of marks and spontaneous techniques. Avoid mechanical repetition; make the texture in your sketch feel like what you are seeing. Be selective.

Feel the mood and atmosphere

One of the great joys of landscape sketching is observing not just the physical landscape, but the effects of weather and atmosphere. The atmosphere of a place strongly affects our perception of it. These effects can be transitory, but what you're seeking with a quick landscape sketch is an impression.

Tips to get you started

1 **What's the weather?** Aside from how weather can affect your materials (mentioned in the last chapter), it makes a big difference to how you approach your sketch. Paint will dry much slower in high humidity. The interesting thing is that a wetter painting (with perhaps even some misting) can be just the thing to convey the wet landscape. In hot, dry weather, you will need to work quickly to spread a wash. Notice how the landscape 'reacts' to bright sunlight, with dramatic contrasts of light and shadow, versus the subtle tonalities of a cloudy, overcast day.

2 **What's the temperature?** As you react to weather you will really use the idea of colour temperature. Allow your feeling of dryness and heat in a landscape to 'colour' your perception; try predominately warm colours in your sketch, regardless of the 'local colour'.

3 **High key or low key?** High key colours are light and bright; low key colours are generally darker and more muted. When we speak of colour saturation, we're talking about how pure and intense it is. Colour with low saturation is muted. A bright sunny day might elicit bright, high key colour, and convey an upbeat mood. On an overcast afternoon, the colours are likely more muted, with little contrast.

4 **Experiment with edges** Notice how sharp, crisp edges convey a very different feeling from soft, 'lost edges'. In bright sunlight, shadows tend to be much sharper, especially where they appear closest to you; sketching or painting sharp edges suggests bright, even harsh light. You get just the opposite effect with wetter techniques; in damp weather your paper will dry more slowly, and that's an opportunity to charge pigment into a damp wash – allowing edges to be soft and diffuse – just as they are likely to appear in the landscape on a wet day.

5 **Ice and snow, heat and sun** Observe how light reacts to snow, and the colour of shadows. Desert heat and bright sunlight will produce different qualities of light and shadow, and will change dramatically over the course of a day. Again, your experience of a place is more than just what you see with your eyes.

Left **Vincent Desplanche, (le Cervin) Matterhorn 4478m, Switzerland, 2015.**
Vincent had only five minutes for this sketch before picking up his daughter from ski school – just enough time for him to convey the light on this famous peak!

Above **Don Low, *Coastal Area at Kyaik Mi Ye Le Pagoda Temple*, Myanmar, 2015.**
Don sketched this scene on a cloudy, windy day. 'When the rain finally arrived, I was painting quickly to avoid being splattered. Surprisingly the sea was calm, and gleaming with the reflection of the bright late morning sky.'

Right **Kris Wiltse, *Olympics from the Port Townsend Ferry*, Washington, USA, 2010.**
Kris did this moody low-key sketch on the ferry. 'It was one crazy ride that day. Sketching was quite a challenge with brushes and palette pitching about. I had to work fast and put down an impression.'

Below **Joyce Hesselgrave,** *San Gabriel Mountains*, California, USA, 2017.
Hiking near her home, Joyce made this pastel sketch on a late afternoon in winter. The hill silhouette grounds the spectacular view of the sky. Notice how softer clouds near the horizon recede in space.

Echo the sky colour in other areas to unify the entire sketch

Notice how the sky is lightest nearer the horizon

Below **Virginia Hein,** *Last Light on the Winter Solstice*, Mojave Desert, USA, 2015.
I was sketching quickly with watercolour, gouache and coloured pencil just as lights began to appear in the distant town. The sky seems to fill the landscape in this flat region of the desert.

Below **Tom Hoffmann,** *Lopez Island, South End*, Washington, USA, 2013.
Tom conveys the feeling of heavy storm clouds with their ominous colours hovering over the landscape. A slice of distant hills and the silhouetted trees focus the drama of the clouds.

Above **Gail Wong,** *Threatening Clouds*, Seattle, Washington, USA, 2015.
In this cloud study, Gail painted with hard and soft edges to convey distant mountains with simple silhouette shapes, and dramatic storm clouds looming directly overhead.

Storm clouds can cast deep shadows on the landscape

Watch the skies

With changing weather comes a vast array of skies – an important aspect of quick landscape sketching. A dramatic sky might easily be a subject in itself! Sketching the sky is another way to express mood, with a dark, storm cloud sky creating a vastly different mood from a clear, cloudless sky.

Tips to get you started

1 **What colour is the sky?** Depending on the weather, the time of day and atmospheric conditions, the colours in the sky will vary dramatically. If you see a bright blue high in the sky, generally the colour becomes lighter closer to the horizon. Look for warmer, yellowish hues, even some red towards the horizon and see the effects of atmosphere. Most importantly, notice how the colour of the sky affects the entire landscape. Echoing the sky colour in areas throughout the sketch helps to unify it.

2 **The colour of atmosphere** Leonardo da Vinci wrote extensively about the way objects far away appear blurred and take on the colour of the atmosphere – the effect of aerial or atmospheric perspective. Da Vinci said that when painting an object 'five times as far away, make it five times as blue'. Pollution and smoke, for instance, will colour distant objects as well.

3 **Show depth** Notice how cloud formations can show depth and distance in a landscape – especially flat, low-lying stratus clouds that, as you see them in the distance, appear smaller closer to the horizon. Note how atmosphere colours distant clouds, and how the edges become more diffuse as well, while clouds that are overhead generally have more distinct shapes. Consider making a low horizon in your sketch to show this effect of depth.

4 **Describe the weather** Clouds can have a dramatic effect on a landscape. Great masses of cumulus clouds hovering over mountains can cast deep shadows; a flat plain can be a stark contrast to the drama of clouds overhead. Storm clouds, with their ominous colouration, give the impression of carrying tremendous weight in water while feathery, bright, luminous clouds high in the sky signal fair weather. Atmospheric conditions colour clouds; haze, dust and fires can turn clouds yellow or red.

5 **Use hard and soft edges** Notice how clouds generally have both hard and soft edges, and the underside of clouds will have very soft colour shadows. With watercolour, try wetting the sky area first, then lightly painting some colour for the atmosphere – a very diffuse, light, warm colour where you want to paint the base of clouds. As the paper begins to dry, paint the sky colour around the cloud shapes, taking care to keep the silhouettes natural and varied. Pastels and other dry media can be used in a similar way, varying the soft and hard edges.

Character of the terrain

Every place on Earth has its own characteristic terrain – a word that describes particular rock formations and other physical features of the earth. The character of the terrain in every region shapes the life of that place – the vegetation, animals and human land use. Observing and sketching landscape begins with recognising those characteristics.

Tips to get you started

1 **Mountains** There is no more awe-inspiring feature of the Earth's surface than mountains, and artists have always been captivated by their drama and grandeur. Notice how the shapes of mountains overlap, with nearer mountains having sharper edges, and those further away appearing softened by the effects of atmosphere. Note how planes in mountains are defined by shadows and light – it helps to 'map' out those areas quickly to create a feeling of depth and volume. The rugged planes of mountains extend towards you in irregular ridges, and appear sharply defined or diffuse, depending on the weather.

2 **Desert** Desert landscape can be varied: the high desert with colourful rock formations in California and Arizona; low desert with wide, vast expanses. You can often see the horizon line; the vastness of the desert has this in common with the ocean. Plants and animals that live in the desert need to be very hardy and resilient, and often take on desert colour camouflage. It may take you a while to become accustomed to desert colour; the greens are often muted, while earth colours can be extremely rich and varied.

3 **Rural landscape** The term 'rural landscape' suggests agricultural fields, farms, rivers. You might see scattered groupings of buildings, fences, roads and other signs of land use, or evidence of historical use, such as abandoned machinery. Choose what you want to focus on; is it the human element with a backdrop of open landscape, or a portrait of the land itself?

4 **Coastal views** These can be very dramatic. A clear view of the horizon as sky meets ocean can be striking. This is a wonderful opportunity to study the effects of atmosphere, as often that horizon is suffused with light and blurred by atmosphere. Choose what most interests you. Is it the view of sea, or the character of the coast itself? You might want to emphasise the vertical drama of cliffs, or the sense of serenity in the horizontal plane of ocean.

5 **Tropical scenes** In a tropical climate, the variety of greens and other colours is almost overwhelming. I remember visiting Hawaii for the first time and feeling overcome by both the intensity of colour and the humidity! Sketching such a scene, I want to express the experience and feeling, with joyous colour and lines.

Above **Don Low**, *Made Becik Waroeng*, Ubud, Bali, 2016.
While Don sat waiting for breakfast at a restaurant overlooking a rice paddy, he made this quick sketch with fine-line marker and watercolour wash, '...simply indicating the light and shadow thrown by the late morning sun'.

The variety of greens and other colours in a tropical landscape can be almost overwhelming

Snow melting on a mountain creates strong patterns of light and dark

Below **Virginia Hein**, *Carson Peak*, Eastern Sierras, USA, 2010.
At high elevations in California's Sierra Nevadas, there's still a lot of snow on mountain tops in June. I was fascinated by the way bright snow etched passages of light on the dark rock face.

Below **Virginia Hein**, *Afternoon View of Opal Mountain*, Mojave Desert, USA, 2010.
Spring in the high desert can be a revelation – there's much more colour than you might expect in the rocks and minerals that form the terrain, and the surprising variety of blooming vegetation.

Below **Shari Blaukopf**, *May Pond*, Baie d'Urfé, Montreal, Canada, 2013.
Fresh spring greens and a spreading canopy give this tree a joyous and welcoming personality. Notice how Shari has created harmony with the range of warm greens, and some contrast in rocks and foliage.

Below **Joyce Hesselgrave**, *Johnson's Pasture*, near Claremont, Los Angeles, USA, 2015.
Joyce made this sketch while hiking near her home. Canopy and branches were built up with ink lines that follow the growth patterns of this beautiful tree and give it weight and presence.

Above **Virginia Hein**, *Gnarled Tree*, Glendale, California, USA, 2010.
I sketched this suburban tree in autumn, struck by the feeling of an aged character, with its sparse foliage and spindly branches, but knowing it would bloom again in spring.

Above **Vincent Desplanche**, *Le Climont 3*, Alsace, France, 1993.
Vincent made a series of sketches while on a hike through the forest. He quickly indicated dark masses of trees with black marker, then added colour and light shining through trees and onto foreground snow with Neocolour.

Focus on trees

Trees are loved for their beauty and variety. Here, we'll consider how to treat trees in the landscape, as well as structure, grouping and forests. How does a tree bring character to the landscape scene? Trees are like principal actors in a landscape, revealing much of the character of a setting.

Tips to get you started

1 **See the forest and the trees** A walk through a forest can be an inspiring retreat. How do you sketch that? This is a good time to pull out the viewfinder and consider whether you want a close-up view or one that encompasses the feeling of a forest wilderness. There are often striking passages of light and dark – dark shadows and silhouettes with flickering light. You may not be able to visually pick out the horizon, but it's helpful to establish it in your sketch, or visualise it on the page as an anchor. You may opt for little or no colour, focusing instead on the play of light and dark patterns.

2 **Different kinds of trees** Pay close attention to the silhouette shape of trees – avoid symmetry and sameness! Be specific about how the character of a conifer differs from that of broad-leafed trees, for example. Each tree is like an individual character with its own personality. Notice the posture of trees, and the way light and shadow mould their forms, as well as the pattern and direction of leaves or needles.

3 **Trees in different climates** Every climate has different kinds of trees, and sketching them is a way of expressing the mood and character of a place. Conifers and other trees in northern latitudes seem to have a ruggedness like the terrain. Sturdy, broad-leafed shade trees, with their spreading canopies, are characteristic of temperate climates. Tropical trees grow lush and vivid green. Palm trees are characteristic of hot climates, water-hoarding cacti of the desert.

4 **Tree studies** To understand the character of trees in a particular landscape, it's very useful to study their anatomy. Observe how a tree's structure can reflect its growth pattern, as well as the pattern created by light that shines through sky holes in branches and foliage. With quick sketching, you won't want to draw every leaf. Look at the overall silhouette shapes of foliage, and how light may pass through some leaves, and masses of leaves in shadow may be very dark. Simplify, but with careful observation of specific branch and leaf shapes, without generalising into a 'generic' tree pattern.

5 **Signifiers of the season** Driving through my neighbourhood in Southern California, I can see that flowering trees have announced spring. Far more reliably than the calendar, deciduous trees signal the seasons. Careful observation of the changes in the life cycle of trees can make your sketches feel in the moment.

Foliage and flowers

Green foliage and vegetation, flowers and other plant life might be the subject of your quick landscape sketch – for example a close-up view, a microcosm of nature with just a few leaves and flowers on a patch of ground. Or, you could use foliage to frame a broader landscape scene and give it depth.

Tips to get you started

1 **The character of foliage** Like trees, foliage can describe a specific terrain and place, as well as the season and climate – sparse foliage with muted colours in a harsh winter landscape, lush foliage and flowers in a tropical landscape or a spring garden in a city. Foliage might be your primary subject in a field of wildflowers, for instance, or perhaps a supporting player in your landscape sketch.

2 **Close-up or far away?** As with trees, you'll want to decide how much to include and how to treat foliage. From how far away are you seeing foliage or flowers? With quick landscape sketching, you will likely want to just suggest masses; this is a good way to create planes of foreground, middle ground or background, with more or less detail according to how close you are. A close-up view could be just the description of an interesting detail, a study of flowers or foliage seen close-up. With distant views, simplify the silhouettes.

3 **Frame your sketch** Foliage can be a good way to frame your sketch, with interesting edges of leaves giving you greenery in the foreground, or the feeling of entering the picture through foliage. Branches can form a pattern or frame through which you effectively view the landscape – defining foreground, with a more distant landscape view in the background. This gives a feeling of depth to your image.

4 **Light on leaves** Leaves are designed to absorb energy from sunlight. As we all probably learned as children, leaves are green because the chlorophyl pigment captures energy from sunlight. Leaves that are high in the tree canopy receive the most light, and tend to be smaller and more delicate. Note the difference in colour, how they seem soaked in light compared to leaves in the interior of the masses of foliage.

5 **Massing foliage and flowers** Branches of trees and bushes naturally grow in bunches or masses, to maximise the surface area receiving light. Wildflowers tend to grow in clusters as well. So, aside from making it easier to sketch foliage and flowers in the landscape, massing these elements will simply look more natural in your landscape sketch.

Right Don Low, *An Old Tree*, Duxton Plain, Singapore, 2014.

Don remembers this banyan as a child on the way to school, seeing it grow larger over the years, now 'a visual delight to me when other types of plants and creepers have grown alongside it'.

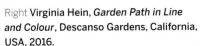

Left Caroline Johnson, *Olive's Hostas*, Devon, 2010.

Sketching in her mother-in-law's garden, Caroline used contrasts of light and shadow to convey bright sunlight, with just the palest washes where sun falls on flowers, and deep shadows underneath.

Right Virginia Hein, *Garden Path in Line and Colour*, Descanso Gardens, California, USA, 2016.

I started with line, just enough to loosely compose the sketch. I painted several layers of colour, massing the foliage, keeping distant foliage as simple shapes, and adding some detail to foreground flowers.

Initial line drawing

Finished sketch

Right **Francis Theo, *Low Tide at Pulau Ubin*, northeast of Singapore, 2016.**
Francis beautifully conveys the sand and rocks of the beach on Pulau Ubin, 'Granite Island', creating texture with ink and wash spatter, dry-brush tapping and dotting with fountain pen.

Left **Laura Murphy Frankstone, *Mt. Hood, Oregon*, Seen from the Snowshoe Trail, USA, 2015.**
Laura sketched the upper portion of Mt. Hood while out snowshoeing with her daughter. The volcanic rock jutting from snow against the brilliant blue sky creates a really dramatic scene.

Right **Laura Murphy Frankstone, *View of the Dolomiti in Italy in October*, 2014.**
Using pencil, watercolour and ink splatters, Laura communicates the drama of the jagged ridges and rugged textures of this 'powerful, surging, ancient landscape' of massive limestone formations.

Light on rocks

I love drawing rocks – the way light defines their surfaces and, like clouds, suggests a fascinating variety of forms. Different kinds of rocks characterise every terrain – layered sandstone and other desert rocks rounded by aeons of erosion, or angular volcanic rocks. For a landscape sketcher, rocks are fascinating surfaces to be suggested with a play of textures.

Tips to get you started

1 **Rock structures** Like mountains, rocks have surface planes; recognising this helps make a sketch with rocks convincing. Whether you are observing rounded, weathered boulders or hard, angular granite cliffs, look for angles and planes. See the large structures first, then add any details of texture, cracks and so forth.

2 **Notice light and shadow** Rock surfaces can seem like a challenging subject, but the key is to look for how light reveals the basic structure, and how their surfaces receive light and shadow. Notice how light tends to fall in patterns and create dimension, as well as where light creates sharp edges or softly rounded shadows.

3 **Depth and distance** Notice how you see the strongest contrasts in any objects, including rocks, that are closest to you. Surface textures, the sharpness of planes, the intensity and variety of colours all appear to diminish with distance, as well as the contrast of light and shadow. Avoid sameness or generalising, even in those distant silhouettes; they are important in describing the character of your landscape.

4 **Surface and texture** A big part of the fun of drawing rocks is the opportunity to play with surface texture. Since we're talking about five-minute landscape sketching here, you want to suggest surface textures rather than render them in detail. Be selective about where you put it. Note how textures and cracks appear to change direction with the shift in planes – use areas of texture to indicate the forms.

5 **What colour is a rock?** This varies with where you are – every terrain and climate has a vast range of rock colours. The colours of the earth vary depending on their mineral composition. For instance, desert sandstone can be brilliant reds due to oxidation, and seem to change colour depending on the time of day. Note the effects of atmosphere on the colours of rocks in different seasons and different times of day. Observing this adds to the richness of landscape sketching.

Urban landscapes

I like to think of an urban landscape as the way a city takes shape and form from the land it inhabits. In the city where I live, views of hills and trees or the ocean are more than a backdrop; they are a reminder that the land that supports the city lives and breathes with life. I always look for that in the places I travel to as well. If you live in a city, you also live in a landscape.

Tips to get you started

1 **Where are you?** A city or town and its landscape takes much from its latitude and climate, elevation, proximity to water and so on. Tropical foliage gives character to a city near the equator, and the city seems to take its colour palette from the surrounding natural environment. The character of the landscape asserts itself in the topography of a city or a town, whether surrounded by mountains or in prairies or deserts.

2 **Nature in the city** Where do you see nature in a city? Trees and other foliage have a way of softening the hard edges of a built environment. In Los Angeles, where I live, tall palm trees stand like sentinels throughout the city, and most neighbourhoods are dotted with all kinds of trees. In an urban landscape sketch, notice the way nature interacts with the city.

3 **The personality of a town** A coastal town with a harbour, a town surrounded by mountains or perched on an island – these places give a town its personality. At the edges of towns, human activity and buildings become sparser. It's interesting to sketch this kind of transitional landscape – roads leading in and out of town.

4 **Buildings in landscape** Buildings are part of all kinds of landscapes. When a building sits alone on stretch of land, we're curious about it – we're often drawn to lone buildings, they signify human habitation in a landscape. As a sketch subject, what do you notice? Does it stand out from its surroundings or seem to blend into the landscape? When sketching buildings in a landscape, notice the angles, and how clusters of buildings sit in relation to each other. Note the functions of buildings – a home, a train station, a church – and also how they relate to the surrounding landscape.

5 **View from a distance** Another way to view urban landscape is to step back, to see a portion of a city or town from a distance. Notice how you can more easily see the way the natural elements and the architecture follow the lines and contours of the landscape forms. From a distance, you can see the silhouette of a city skyline, and how it fits with the natural terrain, sits on a harbour or on top of a hill.

Above **Virginia Hein,** *Downtown Panorama Study*, **Los Angeles, California, USA, 2013.**
The rain had just stopped as the sun began to go down, illuminating the western surfaces of the buildings and turning my distant view into a strong silhouette.

Above **Melanie Reim,** *Gowanus Canal*, **Brooklyn, New York, USA, 2015.**
Melanie sketched the canal on a clean-up day. Once a hub for commercial shipping, '…the turquoise blue of the water is deceiving, the canal is one of the most polluted bodies of water in the United States'.

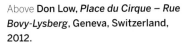

Above **Don Low,** *Place du Cirque – Rue Bovy-Lysberg*, **Geneva, Switzerland, 2012.**
Place du Cirque is a tiny fork junction in the town centre, and Don's sketch shows the way this huge tree gracefully presides over a busy intersection.

Right **Virginia Hein,** *View from the Bluffs*, **Los Angeles, USA, 2017.**
I sketched this midday view with water soluble pencil and watercolour looking westward towards the ocean. The beach towns and the ocean disappear here in great, rolling blankets of fog.

Right **Virginia Hein, *Japanese Garden Bridge*, Descanso Gardens, La Canada, California, USA, 2011.**
The mood here is peaceful, even on a beautiful spring day when many visitors pause for pictures on the bridge. I wanted to show the way visitors become part of the serene atmosphere of the garden.

Below **Virginia Hein, *Rock Climbers*, Joshua Tree National Park, California, USA, 2016.**
The massive rock formations of Joshua Tree National Park attract rock climbers from all over the world; they looked a bit like clambering ants as I sketched them from below.

The further away you place your figures, the less detail you have to include

Below **Marion Rivolier, *Saturday Night in Canal de l'Ourcq*, Paris, France, 2015.**
Marion sketches directly with watercolour shapes. She creates depth by contrasting dark foreground trees with the crowd of people in the middle ground, and softly silhouetted shapes of background trees.

Including figures is a way to animate the scene and give it depth and scale

Figures in landscapes

Figures in a landscape easily become a focal point; they instantly draw the eye, as we tend to identify with a human representation. They literally bring human interest and scale to a landscape scene, and, of course, they are very often simply there – and we sketch them as part of the sense of place.

Tips to get you started

1 **Staffage** The great landscape painters of the 19th century usually included 'staffage' in their sweeping landscape paintings. Staffage are the human and animal figures, usually very small in scale – the fisherman on a lake, the traveller looking up at a waterfall, or perhaps some cows in a field. The figures were not intended as the main subject, simply as a way to animate the scene and give it scale and depth. For me, sketching a gardener at work in a public garden, for instance, adds a human element to the landscape story. The choice is how big a part does the figure play. Does he contrast with the landscape, or seem to be a part of it?

2 **Scale your figures** Consider how important you want the figure or grouping to be in the scene. How large or important is that figure to the story you want to tell? The further away you place figures, the less detail you need to indicate them – just a few gestural marks!

3 **Find a human story** When drawing figures in a landscape scene, consider what the person is doing. This is the best way to convey a sense of life. However, the more detailed and animated the figure is, and the more it contrasts with the

background, the more it draws the eye. Always keep in mind, you can be true to the scene you are sketching while editing; leaving out what doesn't add to your story. How much focus do you want the figures to have?

4 **Figure placement** Finding the horizon line in your sketch (whether or not you draw it) is key to figure placement. If figures are all standing at about the same elevation, they'll line up in about the same place on the horizon (at your eye level). The great illustrator and teacher Andrew Loomis explained it well, stating you can 'hang' your figures on the horizon line. For instance, if you are standing, it's likely that figures will line up through the shoulders or heads (depending on their height). Notice how that changes if you are sitting while sketching.

5 **Animals too** In the same way, consider how animals may either contrast with the background, or appear to blend in. The same goes for size, detail and movement, and what will draw the eye. We'll naturally pay more attention to a large running horse in a landscape than a distant, docile herd of cattle.

Roads, bridges and poles

Unless you are in a true wilderness area, there are always some signs
of human habitation and land use – everything from bridges and roads to
footpaths, telegraph poles and farmland fencing. These things tend to anchor
the landscape for the viewer – something familiar in the natural landscape.

Tips to get you started

1 **Street furniture** In an urban landscape,
'street furniture' refers to all those things
seen on streets and roads, such as lamp posts,
benches, traffic lights and signs. Their presence
in a sketch effectively signals 'city' or 'town', and
gives scale to the scene. In a rural landscape
you're likely to see a hoarding, or a lone road
sign. As the artist, you can edit it out, or you can
include it as a signal of human presence – give
it importance or not. Notice the angles; are you
looking straight on, or are edges angling away
from you?

2 **Notice the path of a road** As mentioned
earlier, paths and roads can literally direct the
eye in your landscape – they imply direction
and movement. A road can act like an arrow
shooting directly at the horizon or slowly
meandering up a hillside. The eye will follow
this path, changing direction, slowing down or
speeding up. Streams and rivers move the
eye in the same way.

3 **Cars and trucks on the road** In a way, cars
and lorries stand in for people in a landscape.
They also are three-dimensional objects, often
highly reflective, and often convey a sense of
movement. How you treat them in the

landscape sketch can vary. A lorry parked by
the side of the road presents solid angles and
planes in the same way a building does, while
cars on a road might be sketched with just a
few lines, suggesting movement and direction.

4 **Fences, pylons and telephone lines** Even in
rural areas, pylons and telephone lines often
dot the landscape, creating a visible network.
Fences may crisscross a landscape. Including
these elements in your landscape sketch can
be a really effective way to show depth and
create direction. Notice how these things
diminish in size as they appear further away,
and how vertical elements like fence posts
appear closer together.

5 **Bridges** Depending on the scale, a bridge
in a landscape can be commanding and
dominate the landscape, or appear natural and
unobtrusive. By definition a bridge is a structure
that carries us across an expanse, and it does
the same in a landscape sketch. The challenge
is to pay close attention to the direction of the
bridge, as well as notice if it arcs or crosses in
a straight line. Like fence posts or telegraph
poles, the vertical pieces will recede back in
space, appearing smaller and closer together.

Left **Virginia Hein, *Travelling Home Through the Desert*, Mojave Desert, California, USA, 2013.**
On the road through Morongo Valley, the road stretches ahead through the desert for many miles, and electricity poles seem to abruptly end as you leave the last town.

Right **Uma Kelkar, *Almaden, Summer*, Almaden Valley, California, USA, 2014.**
The brown landscape of California's Central Valley wine region shows the effect of drought in summer. Uma focused here on the pattern of shadows as well as the rustic fence posts.

Left **Gabriel Campanario, *Puente de Gallocanta*, Montemolín, Spain, 2012.**
While visiting his parents' hometown in southwestern Spain, Gabriel sketched this beautiful old masonry bridge. From his straight-on point of view, he could see the underside of arches in both directions.

Below **Sylvia Shapiro**, *Nancy's Flower Garden*, Vashon Island, Washington, USA, 2002.
Sylvia captures the brilliant colour and light of early summer in a farm garden. Crisp watercolour edges and contrast draw the eye in the foreground, and soft, muted washes in the background create depth.

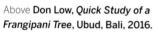

Above **Don Low**, *Quick Study of a Frangipani Tree*, Ubud, Bali, 2016.
Don discovered magnificent views everywhere in Bali, with 'an abundance of trees and tropical plants of every kind', especially frangipani trees. He sketched this vignette at his doorstep just before breakfast.

The window frame provides an interesting contrast to nature glimpsed outside

Left **Caroline Johnson**, *From the Cottage Window*, Elksdale, Cumbria, 2004.
While visiting the Lake District, Caroline sketched this lovely view from her window. The way Caroline has added colour to only the view effectively focuses our attention out of the window frame.

Landscape in a garden

A wonderful way to study nature on a smaller scale is in a garden, often the most accessible places for city dwellers. The character of a garden may be carefully cultivated or wild, but I always like to think that even in an orderly garden, nature has her own way! Here you'll be making decisions about scale – how much to include, and what to focus on.

Tips to get you started

1 **Find nature in the city** Almost every city has parks or green spaces set aside for public use – great places to sketch a landscape that might include a variety of trees and other foliage, as well as figures. Small 'pocket parks' are becoming more common – too small for recreational activity, but they provide a welcome green space in the city, a place to sit outdoors and sketch! Here again, you have the choice of what to focus on. Is it how people interact with nature, or nature itself? You may even have the fascinating contrast of city architecture in your view of the garden.

2 **Botanical gardens** These are great places to do quick landscape sketching. Often you find specialised gardens within the garden, with collections of cacti or tropical plants, and you'll likely have a choice of orderly cultivation or more natural expanses. Some public botanical gardens have media restrictions, so check if you plan to bring more than a basic sketching kit.

3 **Nature in a back garden** Whether a back garden is orderly or wildly overgrown, it offers an opportunity to study nature in microcosm. The landscape is human-scaled, and you want to consider what to include. What is the overall size and shape of the garden? Is it flat or on an incline? These will definitely affect the perspective of your view. Notice overlapping forms of foliage or other features, especially in a somewhat confined space; these will help you achieve a feeling of depth.

4 **Tiny landscapes** One way to approach quick landscape sketching is by creating a vignette – a small image without a definite border. Vignettes are generally most interesting when the edges are irregular. This is great for studies – a close-up view of a few branches, a cluster of flowers or a small garden scene. Consider how you can partially frame it with foliage.

5 **Plants and flowers** When it comes to studying plants and flowers, it's a matter of scale. If you are sketching in a small garden, you may want to focus on just an area. Notice how you will see detail and individual leaves and flowers close-up, and the way those details merge and become simply areas of colour or light and dark contrast when seen from a distance. Your sketch will feel most natural if you only give detail to plants and flowers closest to you, and let those further away become more abstract patches of colour and light.

Painting water

Capturing the fluid quality of water can be challenging, but also exciting! The most important consideration is whether water is moving or still. Since water is essentially transparent, you may see through it, or with still water see surface reflections. Consider what to focus on – just the water or the surrounds as well, which will give context with a shoreline, rocks or foliage.

Tips to get you started

1 **Ocean views** You may need to indicate shoreline and the suggestion of a beach to give context to an ocean view. Notice how the water appears lighter close to shore, taking on the light colour of the sand below, and becomes darker, more bluish with increasing depth. Waves appear to have more contrast of light and dark the closer you are, and lose contrast with the effects of atmosphere in the distance.

2 **Lakes and ponds** It may be the surrounding environment that gives the sketch of a lake or pond meaning – boats, surrounding trees, foliage or buildings. For still, calm water such as lakes and ponds, notice the reflections of surrounding objects. Wind may create movement; ripples on the water will break up reflected images and pick up reflected colours and sparks of light from the environment.

3 **Rushing water** The most important thing to convey here is a sense of movement. You may see the colours of sediment and other things moving beneath the water, but most likely you will see how running water aerates and appears white in areas. It's also likely you'll be painting rushing water in an environment, and the way

it moves over rocks in a stream bed. Notice how you see glimpses of the ground or rocks beneath, and bits of refracted light from the moving water; suggest this by leaving areas of white, as well as following the movement you see with the direction of your strokes. Use a combination of soft and hard edges.

4 **Waterfalls** Here is rushing water seen vertically – most often it appears frothy and white. An effective way of conveying a waterfall is to sketch or paint the surrounding contrast of rocks, allowing much of the waterfall to be negative white space. You want most of all to convey the movement. In a really grand waterfall, you may see expanses of dark rock face contrasting with bright, fast-moving water.

5 **Simplify reflections** Notice how you see slightly more muted colours in the reflections of trees etc., and how forms break up with the light and shadow of ripples. Let your strokes follow the movement of ripples that you see, especially in the foreground. Also pay attention to how reflected shapes will usually have less value contrast; darks appear lighter, while light areas, like the sky, appear darker and duller.

Reflections Red, Reflections Blue,
Seattle, Washington, USA, 2015.
In these studies, Gail practised
'getting a wet wash down first, and
then overlaying the top with hard
strokes' to suggest moving water.
We see light as well as objects
reflected here.

Above **Gail Wong,** *Centre for Wooden*
Boats, Seattle, Washington, USA, 2015.
Gail directs our attention to the bright
patterns of light and shadow reflected in
the water, with strokes in the foreground
following the movement of ripples, and
becoming more muted in shadow areas.

Cool tones reflected in
water break up in a
pattern of ripples

Below **Lynne Chapman,**
Boat Trip from Paraty, Brazil, 2014.
Lynne sketched from the back of a
boat on a home-made accordion fold
sketchbook, unfolding the pages as she
worked, using watercolour and
watercolour pencils. Notice the frothy
wake as the boat cruises between islands.

Warm tones reflect an
object above, then
appear to dissolve in
light further away

Above **Virginia Hein,** *Houses on the Hill*, **Los Angeles, USA, 2012.**
The city's atmosphere (otherwise known as smog!) colours the light, particularly at dusk, when I made this quick sketch just as lights were beginning to come on.

Long shadows in warm light suggest a setting sun

Twilight can be challenging to capture. With an LED headlamp you can see your sketch and palette, and still perceive the colours in your scene

Above right **Joyce Hesselgrave,** *Portland Garden*, **Portland, Oregon, USA, 2016.**
Joyce made this lovely pastel sketch at the edge of a very steep hill with dense forest behind. The late afternoon light created these very dramatic shadows.

Above **Don Low,** *Night at Toa Payoh North*, **Singapore, 2016.**
While dining at a local coffee shop, Don discovered that an ordinary, industrial view became transformed at night, with street lights turning the trees into abstract silhouette shapes, and the sky 'into a blazing ultramarine'.

Left **Virginia Hein, Desert,** *Early Morning*, **Mojave Desert, California, USA, 2016.**
I was up unusually early to see daybreak in the desert, and make a quick gouache sketch before the day heated up. Blues and violets predominate, in clouds, mountains, foreground and even shadows in foliage.

Sketching at different times of day

As Claude Monet did in his famous Rouen Cathedral series, you could paint the same subject over the course of the day and evening, and have startlingly dramatic changes in different lighting conditions. The light and atmosphere of a particular time of day radically affects our perception of a subject.

Tips to get you started

1 **Early morning** Weather and atmosphere can vary dramatically from one place to another, but generally speaking, I find early morning hours to have fairly cool colours, long shadows with a predominance of blues and violets. Values of light and dark are more diffuse – softer and more muted. Many landscape artists and photographers prefer working early in the morning or late in the afternoon, since the light at those times is softer, and colours and shadows more dramatic.

2 **Morning light** Depending on the weather, shadows are long, but become increasingly shorter as you get closer to midday. There's always a temptation to want to 'follow the sun' with your sketch – in other words, change the shadow patterns in your sketch as they change in the landscape. Especially with quick sketching, establish the shadow patterns in your sketch, and don't try to change them!

3 **Midday** Of course, with the middle of the day, depending on the weather, comes the brightest sunlight. The sun is high in the sky and creates sharper light-dark contrast in the landscape, and shadows are short and dark.

4 **Afternoon** As shadows lengthen again, similar to early morning, light conditions change rapidly as the sun descends below the horizon. Again, as the sun moves you want to quickly establish the areas of shadow and light, and don't try to change them. Late afternoon is my favourite time to paint; the light is golden, and I see more colour in shadows.

5 **Twilight into night** Twilight is that time of day just after the sun sets but there's still some light in the sky – sometimes called the 'blue hour', since you can occasionally see a bluish cast of the light. Sketching at this time of day is challenging, but can be a lot of fun, and yield fascinating results! One approach is to start with a dark paper, or paper painted with a dark ground, and add the light as you sketch. I have used a fisherman's headlamp for night sketching – just enough LED light to see my palette and the sketch, but not affect the scene I'm sketching.

Take it further

'Ancora imparo,' said Michelangelo –
'I am always learning.'

In that spirit, here are more ideas and tips to keep you going on your sketching journey. And it is a journey: there is always more to discover and to learn. In this chapter we'll look at ways to stay motivated and excited about quick landscape sketching, and to keep it interesting by challenging yourself to attempting something new or trying it a different way.

Left I reserved negative space around the water tank and tree sky-holes by brushing on masking fluid first, letting it dry and then painting watercolour shapes. Finally I added brown pencil.

Where do you go from here?

Regularly practising landscape sketching has a lot of benefits; very importantly, you develop confidence and trust in your hand and eye. Maintaining a practice of quick-sketching on location is the key to infusing energy and excitement into those larger, more 'finished' works.

Tips to get you started

1 **Drawing is seeing** You'll sometimes hear it said that 'drawing is seeing', because drawing, particularly landscape sketching, begins with observation of your subject. The interesting thing is that it also works the other way: the more you sketch, the more you see. With a regular practice of sketching, you'll see in line, shape and colour relationships, which changes the way you look at the world.

2 **Keep a daily practice** I cannot say enough about the benefit of a daily sketching practice! There's no better way to build and maintain your skill. If I miss too many days sketching, I have to readjust my brain to conquer an initial awkwardness before I feel my drawing 'flow'. I think daily sketching also builds confidence in your skills – a necessary component to growing and developing as an artist.

3 **Strengthen the connection** This is a significant reason to keep a quick sketching 'habit' – it strengthens and maintains an important connection: that between your hand, the tool and the paper, as well as the eye and

the mind (your intention). Another benefit to a daily sketching practice is that observational sketching is linked to the part of the mind that imagines and conceives new ideas.

4 **Be open to new ideas** Once you have developed a skill, and a way of sketching that works for you, it's easy to get a bit stuck in that pattern. Challenge yourself. Give yourself a goal; try sketching in a different way, or try a new technique or medium. There's something exciting and invigorating about working in way that's not completely familiar; you're not quite in control, which can lead to exciting results!

5 **Share with a supportive community** Whether you find a community of fellow sketchers locally or you join an online community, it is a huge benefit to share your sketches. A community keeps you motivated; it's far more challenging to keep your sketching practice going in complete isolation. There's no better way to find new information about tools and materials, see different ways to approach things, and get valuable feedback and encouragement.

Right **Virginia Hein, *Uphill Sketch in Line*, Los Angeles, California, USA, 2015.**
Passenger sketching is something I do whenever I'm lucky to be a passenger. On a weekly drive uphill above the city, the challenge is to sketch the journey differently each time.

Above **Virginia Hein, *Uphill Sketch Ink and Wash*, Los Angeles, California, USA, 2015.**
On a dry autumn morning, the hills and foliage looked golden, and there was a soft blue haze in the sky. I used ink, ink washes and some watercolour.

Below **Virginia Hein, *Uphill Sketch in Mixed Media*, Los Angeles, California, USA, 2016.**
On a morning with strong patterns of shadow and light, I sketched quick masses for foliage with water-soluble pencil, and added some watercolour wash, then layered pencil on top.

Right **Don Low, *Redang Island*, Malaysia, 2011.**
Don sketched this spread while on a snorkelling trip, recording each leg of the adventure, including the sketch of the fish recorded immediately after he returned to the boat.

Below **Liz Steel, *Akaroa*, New Zealand, 2017.**
On a hot day, Liz decided to fill her page with small vignettes rather than a whole scene, and used different media for each, keeping an eye to the overall design of her page as she sketched.

Design multiple views on a page so the eye moves easily between them. Close-ups combined with an overall scene tell a bigger story.

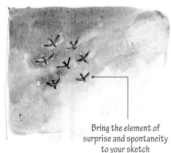

Bring the element of surprise and spontaneity to your sketch

Left **Caroline Johnson, *The Way to the Woods, Birds Flying*, France, 2016.**
As Caroline was drawing the gateway scene, a flock of birds suddenly flew over in perfect formation against the bright blue sky, and she had to capture them! Be ready for those unplanned moments!

Storytelling in your sketch

When you're sketching on location, you're always telling some kind of visual story. Quick landscape sketching can suggest a brief story, even if it's merely a hurried observation. You may not have time to bring a lot of narrative detail to a quick sketch, but there are ways to quickly add to the story.

Tips to get you started

1 **Combine scenes** A great way to expand the story is to combine vignettes on a page – a kind of montage of related scenes. Each little vignette might focus on a different part or aspect of the scene. You could combine a few close-up views of interesting details with a larger view. The way you design the page makes it interesting; sketches can be very casually composed, leaving some white space so each sketch can 'breathe' but still visually relate to one another. The viewer gets a more expanded view of the scene with the combination of images, and visually connects the story.

2 **Create a sequence** Another way to combine multiple images in order to tell more of a story on a page is to draw them sequentially, in the style of a movie storyboard or graphic novel. We generally read from left to right and top to bottom, so we will 'read' a sequence of little sketches the same way. Some borders can be added for clarity.

3 **Add a word or two** Written observations are an excellent way of bringing another dimension of storytelling to your sketches, such as the time of day or other observations about the landscape scene. Even if you don't feel you have a calligrapher's skill for writing or printing, handwriting can add an interesting and personal visual element to your sketch, as well as details that are specific to the time and place.

4 **Choose a detail** With quick landscape sketching, you won't have time to add a lot of detail, but taking some time to select and focus on one particularly interesting detail can tell a great visual story.

5 **Stay in the moment** When you are sketching out on location, you never know what surprising thing can occur. Be ready to bring those wonderful, serendipitous events to your sketch! A flock of birds suddenly takes off, for instance; you probably didn't plan that in your sketch, but see if you can add that surprising element to give your sketch the feeling of immediacy, of truly capturing a moment in time.

Make it your story

When sketching a landscape, it may seem that you are simply recording the 'facts' of the scene – quickly sketching what you see. In truth, we are always seeing landscape through the very personal lens of our own unique senses and experience. With that in mind, consider how you can add more to the story.

Tips to get you started

1 **Add narrative** Writing some quick thoughts or reflections on your sketch not only adds information, but can effectively fix an event in a specific time and place. Consider where you want to add writing as you visualise the scene on your page so it becomes part of the composition. This doesn't have to be formal; informal notes are visually interesting and add another level of storytelling to your sketch.

2 **Make it personal** Sketching and journalling aren't really so far apart. Consider what you could add; a memory or a quick observational note that ties a particular landscape to your life in a personal way lends richness and depth to your sketch.

3 **Collage elements** Collaging sketches with found objects or paper can add a lot to your drawing. You can either include them in advance and allow those elements to suggest the design, or use things found on site as part of the process of creating your sketch. A train ticket from the journey to your landscape site, an object on the ground, bits of paper found at your site – including these kinds of elements can add another level of narrative interest to your quick landscape sketch.

4 **Drawing and handwriting** Calligraphy, the art of decorative lettering, is very close to drawing – it can be formal or loose and casual. Drawing and handwriting are closely linked. However, don't worry if you think your handwriting doesn't look like calligraphy! A written note on a sketch has visual interest along with drawing.

5 **Moment to moment** You can develop an interesting page by sketching a quick little landscape vignette, and then adding another the next day, and the next, finding something different to focus on each day until you fill your page. This can result in some surprising and interesting juxtapositions, as you tell a story over a period of time, designing the page as you go along.

Left Uma Kelkar, *On Way to Manchester*, near Manchester, 2016.
While on a train, views out the window are speeding by, so Uma focused into the distance, 'letting the scenes print' on her mind, as she quickly recorded each little scene.

Below Liz Steel, *Museum of Island Life*, Isle of Skye, 2009.
Here Liz combined several views to tell the story of her visit, including a little top view, her written observations and a quotation. Note the little admission ticket added to the page!

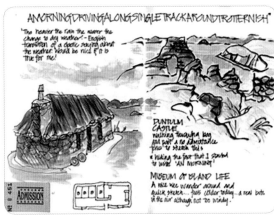

Above Pat Southern-Pearce, *Bronte Moors*, Yorkshire, near the Lancashire border, 2016.
Pat often incorporates her beautiful calligraphy into her sketches. Here it adds visual impact to her spontaneous sketch, and records many lovely details about the afternoon.

Right Virginia Hein, *El Capitan*, Monument Valley Navajo Tribal Park, Utah, USA, 2010.
Monument Valley is unforgettable. I left, taking the stories and the beauty with me. I don't usually write much on my sketches, but I didn't want to forget the story about this landmark.

Right **Virginia Hein,** *October Tree,* Pasadena, California, USA, 2016.

I sat in a courtyard, close by this tree. I was drawn to the tangle of branches emerging from the ground, and the pile of leaves surrounding it, casting a warm, golden shadow upwards.

Below **Melanie Reim,** *One Hundred Views of Haystack Rock 49-53,* Cannon Beach, Portland, Oregon, USA, 2014.

During her three-day visit to Haystack Rock, Melanie made 100 views, each time finding a new and interesting point of view. Notice the eye level in the wonderful sketch at bottom.

Above **Liz Steel,** *Torrin, on the Road to Elgol,* Isle of Skye, 2009.

Parked in a 'passing place', Liz had to be quick with this sketch! She caught the scene with a few lines and watercolour wash, and added a map to show an overview.

A little map of the area can add interest to your sketch as well as being a great exercise in visualising the scene from a different point of view

Right **Virginia Hein,** *Arboretum Turtles,* Arcadia, California, USA, 2015.

I was sketching at the lake in the Los Angeles Arboretum, and noticed this half-submerged log with basking turtles. I stopped to sketch it before the turtles decided to move on.

Try sketching different vantage points and filling your page with different points of view of the same subject

Change your point of view

There's often a tendency to plonk down in a comfortable spot and sketch the first landscape view we see. To break the habit of drawing the 'typical' point of view, try some different and unexpected angles and viewpoints. Do you always sketch sitting down? Try standing up. Find a higher or lower position.

Tips to get you started

1 **Bird's eye view** As the name suggests, this is a view from a high vantage point looking down. It also suggests a view that covers a large area – like an overview. A bird's eye view could be from a mountain lookout, a high window or even an airplane. You are most likely seeing distance, and therefore the effects of atmosphere. Looking down into a canyon, you'll often see atmospheric haze, which changes the colour and clarity, and the same may be true for an urban landscape viewed out of a window. Notice how objects become hazy and indistinct in the distance. The perspective may change, depending on whether you are looking straight down or off in the distance towards the horizon. Note how whatever is closest to you has more detail and contrast than what's further away.

2 **Worm's eye view** What does a worm see? A worm's eye view is a perspective seen from below your subject, and it also implies a humble view. A worm's eye view is not a common view for us. It can be a fresh way to look at the world – seeing things not ordinarily noticed. It might mean looking at a landscape or small creatures at ground level, or looking up. Looking up at a tree from a worm's eye view would make that tree appear especially tall and grand.

3 **Multiple points of view** A great way to really get to know a subject is to look at it from multiple points of view. Again, we often start with the first view we see, and then move on to another scene. Instead, try moving to another vantage point to sketch, repeating the process to fill a page with different points of view of the same subject; you will really get to know that tree or rock or whatever you choose in a very different way.

4 **Narrow your focus** You choose a view and perhaps sketch whatever fits comfortably on your page. What if you were to crop that image, to focus on just the most interesting aspect of the scene? This is something that gets easier to do as you begin to see your subject as shape. You might notice an interesting juxtaposition of shapes or colours occurring in one area of your view. What if you focused only on that?

5 **Map it out** Sometimes a quick little overview map can add interest to your sketch – providing another piece of information about your landscape scene. This is a great exercise in visualising the scene from a different point of view. Don't worry if it's not exactly to scale!

Experiment with formats

If you find that you typically work on the same size and format – always horizontally, for instance – a good method to expand the way you see and sketch landscape is to experiment with different formats. Try turning the page, or choosing a different sketchbook format.

Tips to get you started

1 **Vertical formats** A 'landscape format' in page orientation and photography is by definition horizontal, and that's how we typically think of landscapes. However, you shouldn't feel limited by that! Shifting your focus to a vertical format can dramatically change the way you think about a landscape, and it's actually ideal for many subjects. Consider how you might make a tall tree the focal point of your sketch, or a sky of dramatic clouds, or billowing smoke; it creates a very different visual story. Consider where you place the horizon in your sketch. Is the story about something in the foreground, or further in the distance, like the drama of clouds in the sky before a storm?

2 **Panoramas** Take the idea of a horizontal format and expand it outward to a 'wide-angle' view on a horizontal page. The view of a waterfront, for instance, or an urban skyline, are ideal subjects for a panorama format. In most compositions you would have one major focal point. In a panorama, you might have more than one – as a way to move the eye back and forth. Typically when sketching, you would include no more than what you can see without moving your eyes or turning your head (your field of view). With a panorama, you might break the rules!

3 **Accordion fold** This sketchbook format lends itself to several possibilities. Since it opens panel by panel, it might work for sequential storytelling, multiple views or a way to record daily changes in the landscape.

4 **Go bigger** Working larger is worth mentioning here because artists so often feel that their initial sketch of a scene captures a sense of life and energy, precisely because it was done quickly and often on a small scale. The trick is to maintain that same energy as you move to a larger format. Starting with those important first few minutes of careful observation, select and identify the important shapes and simplify. Often it's also about keeping the same feeling of freedom and exploration in the marks you make as you move to a larger scale.

5 **Redesign your page** We have tendency to accept the dimensions of the page as 'law' – that we have to fill that space. Instead, consider the page as yours to design. Think about where negative space will allow the viewer to fill in the rest of the scene. Or, begin with a border that may or may not echo the dimensions of the page, creating your own boundaries on the page with an eye to the overall design.

Below **Virginia Hein,** *Panorama in the Wind*, **Joshua Tree National Park, California, USA, 2013.**
Joshua Tree National Park contains vast expanses, and I felt I needed a panoramic view to give a sense of the immense scale.

Right **Kris Wiltse,** *Methow River, near Carlton, USA, 2010.*
Kris creates a vertical panorama here. Notice how she created multiple points of view, from the foliage right in front, following the flow of the river upwards to the horizon and the distant mountains.

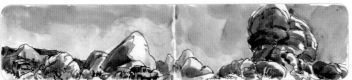

An accordion fold sketchbook is a lot of fun when sketching multiple views or recording daily changes in a landscape

The pages unfold panel by panel to reveal the story

Above **Virginia Hein,** *360 Degree View of Hidden Valley*, **Joshua Tree National Park, USA, 2017.**
I used a 48-page accordion-fold sketchbook to sketch a view I've sketched many times, but this time, wanted to see if I could make a 360 degree view. I just made it!

Below **Virginia Hein,** *View from Montjuic*, **Barcelona, Spain, 2013.**
Every sketcher who visits Barcelona sketches the great La Sagrada Familia. I happily discovered this bigger picture – a distant view with La Sagrada rising above the city, yet surrounded by mountains.

Above **Joyce Hesselgrave, *Sunset in Claremont*, California, USA, 2017.**
Joyce made this beautiful sketch with pastel near dusk after a rainy day, with the clouds moving and changing shape. Pastel is ideal for blending soft, atmospheric effects quickly.

Below **Virginia Hein, *Waterfall, Descanso Gardens*, La Canada, California, USA, 2015.**
A calligraphy brush pen is a great tool for super-quick sketching. You can create a range of marks from delicate to bold, and it's a good exercise in pushing values to black or white.

Brush pens and markers can be great for quick landscape sketching and will react in different ways on different papers

Above **Gary Geraths, *LAX Trees Lot 5*, Los Angeles, California, USA, 2010.**
Gary made this little gouache painting looking towards the airport from the top of a parking garage in late afternoon. The scale feels large with his use of big, bold shapes and colour.

Below **Virginia Hein, *Descanso Garden Gouache Studies*, La Canada, California, USA, 2016.**
These are thumbnail-sized sketches made with gouache – very different from transparent watercolour, as I work with mostly opaque layers. I massed the shapes of foliage, and suggested summer flowers with spots of colour.

Working small with a large brush helps simplify the painting

Focusing on a detail, keep it loose

Detail in foreground contrasts with atmospheric background

Explore different media

The variety of media available to you as a sketcher is endless! Here are some suggestions – a rudimentary list of media to consider as you expand your sketching practice. New media is becoming available all the time, especially with the growing number of location sketchers!

Tips to get you started

1 **Pastel** This is a wonderfully rich medium that lends itself well to quick landscape sketching, as the application is direct; you can achieve rich colour effects very quickly. However, it can be messy. There are two types of pastels: dry pastels and oil pastels. Both will give you rich, direct colour but otherwise have different working qualities. Soft, dry pastels are chalky and are blended as you work. Oil pastel can be blended on the page with turpentine or similar solvent, or left direct so that your marks are clear. Some artists who work with pastel carry a small can of fixative (dry and oil pastels take different types of fixative). Fixative doesn't work completely, however, so use a separating sheet (glassine, tracing or parchment paper) between drawings on location to minimise smearing.

2 **Paint with gouache** Gouache can be used thinly like transparent watercolour, or much more thickly and opaquely. It works well for quick sketching, especially if you keep the scale small. Note that light colours often dry a little darker, and dark colours sometimes dry lighter.

3 **Colour inks** Some colour inks are suitable for fountain pens, others work better for dip pens. India ink and other heavier body inks can clog a fountain pen, so only use them with dip pens or bamboo pens, or for brush drawing. Inks can be permanent or water-soluble. Colour ink is exciting because the colour is often super-saturated, and can be diluted to make a lovely wash drawing. Inks that resist water are labelled 'document', 'waterproof' or 'permanent'.

4 **Brush pens and markers** Brush pens can be felt tip or have a little brush, waterproof or water-soluble. Brush pens and markers are great for very direct mark-making and colour. Markers will react in dramatically different ways on different types of paper, and come in several formulas, from traditional alcohol- or solvent-based markers to, more recently, pigment and watercolour markers. Alcohol and solvent markers are considered 'permanent', but the dye colours eventually fade; newer pigment markers stay bright.

5 **Try a resist** There are all kinds of ways you can work with resists for some interesting results – a quick and easy way to 'reserve the white' of your paper when working with watercolour. The classic method is to use any kind of wax – candle wax, white crayon etc. You can also use masking fluid, designed to be peeled off once paint is dry, or the 'permanent' type, which leaves a textured effect.

Water-soluble media

Water-soluble media is a topic in itself! It can be exciting, although it
takes some practice to work comfortably with any kind of water-soluble media.
You will want to experiment with how much water to use and where to use it.
There's a certain level of unpredictability with water-soluble media,
which is part of the fun and likely the reason for its popularity.

Tips to get you started

1 **Water-soluble crayons and pastels** I've long
enjoyed working with water-soluble crayons
and, more recently, water-soluble pastels
because it feels like drawing and painting at
the same time – or, more precisely, alternately
drawing and painting. It's a great medium for
quick landscape sketching, since it can give you
fresh, spontaneous results. With practice you
gain control over how much to blend and where
to leave your marks. The trick is not to 'over-
blend' – you don't want all your expressive
marks to disappear. Blend selectively, or work
back into a wet sketch to get strong, juicy
marks and texture.

2 **Watercolour pencils** Similar to watercolour
crayons, these work best with a layered
approach – sketching and laying in some values
with pencil strokes, and then selectively
applying some water or watercolour. Be
prepared for some colour surprises! Most
watercolour pencils will become much brighter
in colour when you apply water.

3 **Watercolour sticks** These are highly
concentrated pigment and can be used on
either wet or dry paper, although I think they
are most effective and rich on wet or damp
paper. They can also be wetted with a brush in
the same way you'd work with pan
watercolours.

4 **Watercolour graphite** One of my favourite new
media is watercolour graphite, which comes in
a pan or stick form. With the pan, I like to mix a
small solution of water with the graphite for a
middle-value wash along with working directly
with brush into the pan. What's interesting
about this medium is that you get a granular
mix of graphite for some surprising textural
effects. I like this particularly for sketching
rocks – it's a very rock-like texture. Water-
soluble chalk sticks are also interesting for the
earthy textures and tones. Working in broad
strokes is a nice counterpart to a fine line.

5 **Draw on a wet page** This is another way to
work with water-soluble crayons, pastels,
pencils and chalks – work directly onto a wet
page, or into a wet painting. The marks will be
strong, bold and lively – and unpredictable!

Water soluble pigment blocks can be applied on dry or damp paper – the big, blocky shape is great for bold, expressive sketching.

Watercolour sticks used here on dampened paper. The colours are richer and apply more easily than on dry paper.

Above left **Lynne Chapman**, *Red Wharf Bay*, Anglesea, Wales, 2013. Lynne made this quick sketch on an empty beach, drawing while standing up, with a small selection of watercolour pencils and a water brush. Notice how some areas are blended, but she allowed her expressive pencil strokes to remain.

Above **Virginia Hein**, *Norton Simon Museum Garden*, Pasadena, California, USA, 2016.
I sketched the last afternoon light in this lovely garden, where I couldn't bring a full watercolour set. Therefore, I used watercolour pencil and water brush to blend, adding more pencil line for texture.

Watercolour pencil with water added can create surprising colour shifts – usually much more saturated colour!

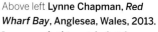

Right **Virginia Hein**, *360 Degree View of Hidden Valley (Close Up)*, Joshua Tree National Park, USA, 2017.
Here is an enlarged view of four pages of the accordion-fold sketchbook shown previously. I used ink for line, and watercolour graphite for shadows; it naturally granulates and creates a mineral texture.

Right **Melanie Reim**, *First and Last Impression*, Canon Beach, Portland Oregon, USA, 2014.
You can really feel the excitement of waking up to this spectacular view in Melanie's sketch! Here she layered pencil, watercolour and gouache to create rich surface texture.

Below **Virginia Hein**, *Desert Drive Home*, Highway 62, Mojave Desert, California, USA, 2015.
This sketch started with big watercolour and gouache shapes of mountains looming over the highway; then I felt it needed some bright highlights and definition, so added a few coloured pencil strokes.

Above **Virginia Hein**, *Water Tank View*, Los Angeles, California, USA, 2017.
In this sketch of a nearby hill, I started with pencil on tan paper, then added white crayon to bring light to the sky, which created a resist for the watercolour wash.

Layer with mixed media

A great thing about quick landscape sketching is that it's an opportunity to experiment. Explore mixed media and layering. The experiment is in how you layer, what you put on top of what. An experimental attitude and sustained practice will expand your skills and your confidence level!

Tips to get you started

1 **Let the fun begin!** I don't always start out with the idea of layering in a quick landscape sketch – sometimes it just happens! With quick landscape sketching you are trying to capture a place and feeling quickly, with spontaneity. Of course, you can overdo it; but every time you 'overdo' a sketch, perhaps adding one layer or colour too many, you learn something that you wouldn't learn any other way. If you view sketching as an opportunity to experiment and learn, then you will fall in love with the process and likely be happier with the results!

2 **Think in layers** While I strive to follow the patterns of light I see in the landscape, sometimes it can get lost, and then I want to work the light back into the sketch. The key here is to add the light with white or colour gouache or white pen as another layer – although less is more! Add it in more than one place so that it looks intentional, not like an attempt to 'correct a mistake'. I might use a pencil to 'carve' a line into a damp wash to add emphasis and clarity. Anticipate where you'll want to take a layered approach, but keep an open mind to an inspiration. Use layering to suggest distance and atmosphere, leaving the foreground with sharper contrast.

3 **Be selective** A layered approach to sketching can become muddy, especially when you are working with opaque media. Be selective about how and where you want to layer. This is also where testing your pigments in advance is useful; notice how some pigments with white or earth colours will cover a transparent layer quickly, but too many layers become muddy. Consider what you can refine with layering. Sharpen or soften edges? Separate planes?

4 **Something for now, more later** Often the best use of your quick sketching time is to take a few minutes to select your subject, consider the optimal point of view, and make a quick drawing in ink or pencil, with a plan to come back later. If you can return the same time of day, so much the better, although there's no guarantee that the weather conditions will be identical. Let the new situation dictate the end of the sketch.

5 **When is it enough?** Knowing when you've taken a sketch just far enough is not an easy thing to learn, and often learned by going too far! I find it most often happens when I lose focus. Push it as far as you can while you are in the 'flow' of working, but stop *before* you start to second-guess yourself or lose interest.

Improvise with what you find

A great thing about quick sketching a landscape on location is that there's often an abundance of materials that can be incorporated into your sketch. A carton or box can be sketched on. Using an element of what you find on site can connect you to the landscape in a different, more personal way.

Tips to get you started

1 **Be resourceful** What if you arrive at your chosen landscape location and discover you've forgotten some favourite material? (I've done it myself!) There could be any number of alternatives here. Anything that produces some colour can be used for painting: tea, wine, coffee – the list could go on! A child's crayon set, biros, cotton buds, chopsticks; sometimes using unconventional materials can bring forth interesting problem-solving!

2 **Using natural materials** Pigments have, of course, been made from natural materials since anyone first made paint, and sticks and other found objects have been used to draw or apply pigments. There's something wonderful about connecting to this ancient practice. I have collected beautiful, soft red earth from the Arizona desert, sifted it through a fine mesh and added distilled water, gum arabic as a binder and other ingredients to create pigment. This takes some experimentation to create a workable consistency – look online for a variety of recipes. Or try incorporating earth into your paint as you work.

3 **A stick and some ink** A stick found on your landscape site may be sharpened or used as is as a great drawing tool when dipped into ink. The line you produce will be organic and somewhat less predictable than with a manufactured tool.

4 **Anything that makes a mark!** Besides a stick, you're apt to find all kinds of things that can be used as drawing or painting tools. I have found old, rusty nails in the Mojave Desert near a homestead cabin and used them to dip into ink and watercolour – something I found very satisfying, knowing that the tool came from the landscape that I was sketching.

5 **Paint with what's at hand** I've had fun experimenting with coffee – mixing instant coffee to a syrupy consistency, and diluting it for golden brown washes, which is somehow very harmonious with landscape painting. If you've ever had 'cowboy coffee', that heavy brew cooked over a campfire, now you know what to do with the dregs!

Right Virginia Hein, *Painting with Coffee at Stirrup Tank*, Joshua Tree National Park, USA, 2017.
I'd heard about painting with instant coffee, and just had to try it! The darks required a syrupy consistency, and I diluted it for washes. It smelled good, too!

Left Virginia Hein, *Mojave Desert*, near Twentynine Palms, California, USA, 2012.
Inspired to find something on site to sketch with, I found rusty old nails near an old house, which I dipped in watercolour for the lines, and used a Chinese brush for washes.

Below Ch'ng Kiah Kiean, *View of Danshui*, Taiwan, 2011.
Kiah Kiean is well known for his panoramic drawings made with twig and Chinese ink. He borrowed a twig from a friend, Prof. Chen, to make this first sketch, and fell in love with the quality of line.

Below left **Pat Southern-Pearce, *On the M6 Motorway*, Stafford, 2016.** Passenger-sketching on a rainy day, Pat sketched the racing clouds with water soluble drawing media used dry, and opaque white pen for highlights and lettering on black sketchbook paper.

Drawing on colour or toned paper can prompt a fresh direction in your approach

Right **Laura Murphy Frankstone, *Arctic Norway, Sketched from a Moving Boat*, Norway, 2013.** Laura sketched with watercolour crayon and graphite on toned paper to capture the atmosphere of the polar night, a period in Arctic Norway in which the sun doesn't rise above the horizon.

Drawing or painting with light is very effective on a black ground, especially for conveying a night-time or early morning illumination

Above right **Pat Southern-Pearce, *In the Black Forest*, Germany, 2016.** 'Scribbling madly, in the car as light was beginning to fade,' Pat sketched the snowy forest on yellow paper with fountain pens, colored pencils and a white pen.

Left **Virginia Hein, *Pink Sunset*, Mojave Desert, California, USA, 2017.** The light of high desert skies can be overwhelming. For this gouache sketch I experimented with a pink ground to show the soft, pink glow at sunset.

Try a different ground

Most sketchbooks have white paper, and that is simply what most of us are used to. Watercolour is traditionally painted on white paper, and reserving the white of the paper is how you retain the brightest light. However, using colour or toned papers can bring an interesting dimension to quick landscape sketching.

Tips to get you started

1 **Mood with a mid-tone value** When you are in a relatively low-light situation – early morning, early evening or an overcast day – a mid-tone paper is a great way to begin a sketch with a sense of mood. The difference is that you intentionally bring in the light, using white or other light colours.

2 **Start with a colour ground** The dimension of colour immediately brings mood and emotion to a sketch, and it's an interesting challenge to start with a colour paper or ground. Whether you start with a cool colour or a warm colour, notice how that affects any colour you put on top. Depending on the colour, you will likely be adding the lightest light, as well as some darker values.

3 **Repurposed paper** Many artists enjoy sketching on 'repurposed' paper – old notebooks, graph paper, maps and all kinds of printed papers, even old sketches. This can be an interesting challenge, or may prompt a fresh direction in your sketch.

4 **A different surface** A texture like sandpaper is often used with pastel, for the 'bite' of the surface. Watercolour grounds can be applied to just about any surface to make them absorbent and 'paintable', although my experience is that it seems to work better for heavier watercolour or gouache than for light, transparent effects. Other materials, such as sand, can be added to a ground for textural effects.

5 **From black to light** Starting with black paper or painting on a surface with a dark ground is a wonderful way to do a night scene! Artists have long used dark grounds for oil painting, in order that light 'emerges' from the painting, rather than being the starting point. Drawing or painting with light is very effective on a black ground, especially for conveying scenes of night-time illumination.

Catch a singular moment

This is frequently at the heart of quick sketching – there are some moments that only happen once, and you are lucky to be there to sketch them! This is so often true of landscape sketching, since you will never see the exact same landscape twice. The weather, the season, the time of day or any number of other factors can change the landscape in any particular moment.

Tips to get you started

1 **You had to be there** Location sketching can be a case of 'you had to be there'. Perhaps something extraordinary happens, or something I have often found – that I've been in a certain place and made a sketch only to discover later that the place is gone! Parkland can been built on, or any number of things can change the face of the landscape. This is something that makes location sketching so special; you are witnessing something with your sketch that may never happen again.

2 **You have only five minutes!** Sometimes you are in situations where you have no choice: sketch it now or it's gone! Or, you might have impatient companions, or maybe the train is leaving – lots of things can compress your sketch time. This is the time for quick decisions. What can you get down quickly that will make the most of this moment?

3 **Once in a lifetime** And then there are singular events – a once in a lifetime solar eclipse, or seeing the Aurora Borealis or some other incredible natural phenomena. If you have your materials at the ready, and with practice in making those quick decisions of what to include

and what to leave out, you can go for it! Don't worry about catching it 'perfectly'; there is something special about the energy of simply being there and sketching in that moment.

4 **Catch the unexpected** You might be working on a sketch and something completely unexpected occurs. A convocation of golden eagles flies overhead; a great blue heron lands ten feet from where you are standing. Again, don't worry about capturing it 'perfectly'. Focus on catching the movement or the activity of what is going on. I was once sketching a distant hillside and suddenly saw plumes of smoke – some brush had caught fire! I was relieved to see that almost instantly there were firefighters on the scene, including a helicopter! I felt compelled to sketch the scene. Thankfully the fire was put out quickly, and I sketched the smoke and firefighters in action.

5 **Go with it!** Don't become self-critical at this point; you aren't necessarily after a perfect illustration of the event. The energy and urgency of a singular moment can communicate beautifully in the way you sketch it – with energy and life.

Above **Gary Geraths, *FIRE Claremont 2*, Claremont, California, USA, 2004.**
Gary painted a raging forest fire on Mt. Baldy from his rooftop in the middle of the night. 'The fires roared down the canyons and lit up the skies with red billowing smoke.'

Right **Laura Murphy Frankstone, *Fumeroles near Lake Myvatn*, Iceland, 2012.**
Laura sketched this dramatic scene with watercolour crayon and graphite on toned paper. 'Steam plumes are part of the primordial energy visible everywhere in Iceland.'

Below **Virginia Hein, *Blimp*, Los Angeles, California, USA, 2009.**
It was late afternoon, and I was sketching a view of downtown Los Angeles. Just as I was packing up to leave, a blimp came sailing overhead, and I hurried to capture it!

Right **Vincent Desplanche,**
Le Climont 2, **Alsace, France, 1993.**
With black marker and a few strokes
of Neocolour crayon, Vincent quickly
established strong value contrasts with
bold shapes in his sketch, allowing the
white of the paper to create dramatic
negative space.

Below **Virginia Hein,** *Japanese Garden
View #1*, **Huntington Gardens, San
Marino, California, USA, 2011.**
I challenged myself to draw a series
of 'green scenes' without using green
pigment. Here I used a limited
watercolour palette of cobalt blue,
Payne's grey, quinacridone gold and
burnt sienna.

*Limit your palette
to a few well-chosen
colours to create
unity throughout
your sketch*

*Push the values that
you see in the scene
for dynamic contrast*

Below **Virginia Hein,** *View
from Barnsdall Park Value Study*,
Los Angeles, California, USA, 2013.
I made this quick study on a hazy
afternoon using values of one
colour (Payne's grey). Working in
monochrome makes it easier for
me to separate planes of foreground,
middle ground and background.

*Working in monotone
makes it easier to see
the range of values in
your scene*

Switch it up!

As you sketch more, you may notice patterns in the way you work. Perhaps you've settled into a comfortable routine in the way you sketch, which is not necessarily a bad thing. However, I often hear sketchers mention things they do consistently but feel they want to change. That awareness is the way you grow as an artist. Push yourself – change the process.

Tips to get you started

1 **Notice your patterns** We all have patterns in the way we approach things, and sketching is no exception. What kinds of things do you notice that you consistently do that you feel you want to change? Some of the most common patterns that I've observed sketchers wanting to change include a tendency to jump into details before recognising the large shapes in a scene; having a lack of value contrast so everything is the same mid-value, and feeling that colours are not unified. First recognise the tendency, then switch up the pattern.

2 **Break your own rules!** If you have a tendency to, for instance, over-focus on details and not see the large shapes in the landscape, try a different approach. Perhaps start with a tool, such as a large brush, that 'forces' you to find large shapes, and then reserve details for later, as you feel you really need them.

3 **Ask yourself questions** Frequently the way to shift the way you work is simply by asking yourself questions. The answer may not always be instantly forthcoming, but the interesting thing is that asking the question opens the door. If, for instance, you notice that your sketches lack value contrast, ask yourself how you can push the values. This may begin with paying particular attention to the contrast of values in your scene, especially the shadows and light within areas of colour. Perhaps it's allowing more negative space into the composition, or mixing paint with a greater range of density than you're used to.

4 **Do the opposite** There's something very powerful about taking a pattern and doing the opposite. For example, if you notice a lack of unity in the colours you choose, try limiting your palette to merely a few well-chosen colours. Whether you mix on the palette or mix on the page, you can achieve a surprising range with just a few colours, leading to a unified sketch.

5 **Honor your own process** Discouragement and frustration and can accompany a feeling of 'not making progress', which can be enough to make some people give up sketching. Don't give up! Honour your own individual process. While you are working it is often necessary to reserve judgement until later, and then consider what you would do differently next time. There is no 'finish line' in sketching.

Next steps

No matter how much you've honed your skills, there is always more to learn and new ways to challenge yourself! I'd like to leave you with a few suggestions about continuing on with quick landscape sketching, as well as taking that quick-sketch attitude further in your work. Do date your sketches – it's important to keep track of your work, and notice the progress!

Tips to get you started

1 **Try it again!** The attitude of quick landscape sketching – of experiment and exploration – is so useful, because it can help you bypass the inner critic that every artist knows all too well. Before thoughts of 'failure' enter your mind when your sketch doesn't come out how you'd hoped, jump into the next one! Pick a favourite view and see how many different ways you can portray it – monochrome or limited palette, watercolour or pencil. Change the tool, change the approach, try a different point of view. See your subject with line, shape, colour, value. Learn from these quick sketches.

2 **Give yourself a time challenge** Do you have a favourite subject? What if you set yourself the challenge of sketching a certain number of trees in a week? Or perhaps you could only draw with pencil for a week. This is a great way to build skills and stay motivated. If you're connected with an online sketching community, you'll see similar sketching challenges.

3 **Sustain a theme** Going further could mean telling a bigger story. Use those quick landscape sketch decisions to do more sustained work. With continuous practise

in quick landscape sketching, those decisions become more instinctive; you start with selection, seeing the shapes and noticing what interests you very quickly, and most importantly, you learn to trust those quick decisions. This is very important to maintain in larger works, and works where you commit quite a bit more time. Picture-making is always about making those decisions as you work.

4 **See beauty everywhere** For a landscape sketcher, this isn't so very hard! As mentioned at the beginning of this chapter, drawing is about seeing, and the more you draw, sketch or paint, the more you will see all around you. You will see beauty in the most unexpected places. A landscape that to the casual observer may look bland and uninteresting can be illuminated by your attention to it, as you interpret that view in line, shape, colour and texture.

5 **There is always more** More to see, more to learn, more to understand! For me, sketching is absolutely soul-satisfying, and I truly wish that experience for you. Please keep sketching and recording what you experience with your own heart, mind and point of view!

Below **Virginia Hein**, *Winter Trees*, **La Canada, California, USA, 2012.**
Two sycamores growing in a parkway; I have drawn them in fall with golden leaves, but here I enjoyed the fragile beauty of just a few seedpods clinging to bare branches.

Above **Shiho Nakaza**, *Dusk: Cloudy Day*, **Playa Vista, Los Angeles, California, USA, 2017.**
Shiho made a series of small watercolour sketches of the same scene. In each, she observed a particular time of day, with different weather conditions; no two scenes are the same.

Left **Virginia Hein**, *Grey Palm*, **Glendale, California, USA, 2013.**
Where I live, palms are everywhere, like sentinels watching over the city. I draw them all the time. I saw this palm from a coffee shop window on a damp, grey morning, and made a quick wash sketch.

Below **Shiho Nakaza**, *Lunchtime: Overcast Day*, **Playa Vista, Los Angeles, California, USA, 2017.**
Shiho sketched this series from a patio at her work, at lunchtime or after work. It's so important to make time and opportunity to sketch the landscapes that are all around you.

By giving a view your attention you can illuminate its beauty as you interpret the colours, shapes and textures of the scene before you

Key Elements

Here are some key elements in landscape sketching, along with a few ways to approach your subject. Understanding these elements can help you find your point of view and simplify your approach to capturing the essence of a landscape scene more quickly.

See direction of bridges and roads

Arch bridge
As a bridge comes toward you, the angle changes the shape of the arc and you see some underside.

Suspension bridge
In a large bridge, the structure recedes back in space and vertical pieces appear smaller and closer together.

Find your view

Buildings and other structures in landscape

Depth and vanishing points
Sketching a building at an angle helps to show depth. From the angle you're viewing, notice how lines appear to converge at two 'vanishing points' along the horizon line – it helps to visualise this.

Horizon line
Your eye level

Vanishing point

Horizon line
Your eye level
Vanishing point

Vanishing point

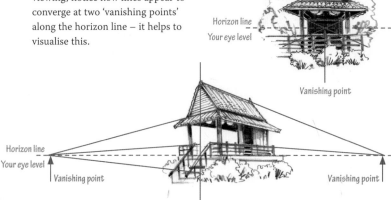

Framing your view
Use the 'viewfinder' to select a view. Try different formats – horizontal, vertical, close-up or a scene with depth. Don't try to copy the view; let your eye and imagination compose the sketch!

Some watercolour techniques

Glazing
Layering one colour over another, usually dry – works best with transparent colours.

Two colour wash
A wash gradation of two colours on damp paper. Allow colours to bleed in the middle; once paint is dry, leave it alone!

Wash gradation
A wash gradation on cold press paper – works best when paper is damp and on a slight slant. Spread wash with a damp brush.

Spattering
Spattering on damp paint for texture.

Flat wash
Shown here on rough paper – use a big brush with plenty of paint, and your paper on a slight slant. Lay in wash with even, horizontal strokes.

Painting clouds
Here, painted wet into wet: paint applied to damp paper, allowing some edges to dry for some contrast to soft, wet washes.

Simplifying foliage

Simplify by massing the shapes of foliage

Quick-sketching foliage
Simplify by focusing on strong silhouettes and contrasts. Look for patterns of light and shadow to help you mass shapes in foliage.

See form and depth

Rocks and streams
Look for the direction of light – depending on the surface, planes may be sharply defined or softly rounded. Notice how light reveals forms and textures.

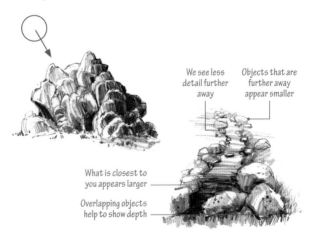

We see less detail further away

Objects that are further away appear smaller

What is closest to you appears larger

Overlapping objects help to show depth

Index

Acknowledgments

Author Acknowledgments

I would like to thank RotoVision for the opportunity to write about something I love, especially editors Nick Jones, Emily Angus and Abbie Sharman, and the talented designers who put this book together.

Thank you to each of the superb contributors who agreed to participate and lend your beautiful work to this book – I am very grateful and honoured!

Thank you to all of my teachers; beginning with my mother Jeanne, my beloved college drawing mentor John Lincoln, and so many others. Thanks also to all of my students, who have also been my teachers, for challenging me and showing me new ways to think differently every day.

I'm deeply indebted to Urban Sketchers, the worldwide community of sketchers who 'see the world, one drawing at a time'. Becoming a part of this very generous and supportive community has changed my life.

Most especially I thank my partner in life, Bill, for his love, his patience, and his insights. He has often observed me sketching, about to overdo it, and said in the immortal words of Dr. Frankenstein, 'Leave it alone, Fritz!'

Picture Acknowledgements

Banh, John 49
doodledose.com

Blaukopf, Shari 13, 21, 28, 32, 41, 58, 70, 78
blaukopfwatercolours.com

Campanario, Gabriel 18, 54, 89
estudiocampanario.com

Capecchi, Simo 70
inviaggiocoltaccuino.com

Chapman, Lynne 93, 111
lynnechapman.net

Desplanche, Vincent 73, 78, 120
vincentdesplanche.com

Frankstone, Laura Murphy 24, 65, 82, 116, 119
laurelines.com

Geraths, Gary 108, 119
garygerathsart.com

Hesselgrave, Joyce 74, 78, 94, 108
joycehesselgrave.com

Hoffmann, Tom 14, 17, 41, 45, 53, 57, 74
hoffmannwatercolors.com

Johnson, Caroline 24, 31, 46, 81, 90, 100
carolinejohnson.org

Kelkar, Uma 38, 49, 89, 103
umakelkar.com

Kiah Kiean, Ch'ng 115
kiahkiean.com

Low, Don 46, 73, 77, 81, 85, 90, 94, 100
donlow-illustration.com

Miles, Judith Alsop 31
jamilesart.com

Nakaza, Shiho 35, 49, 57, 123
shihonakaza.com

Reim, Melanie 27, 70, 85, 104, 112
sketchbookseduction.blogspot.com

Rivolier, Marion 57, 86
marionrivolier.fr

Shapiro, Sylvia 90
sylviashapiro.wordpress.com/author/sylviashapiro

Shirodkar, Suhita 38, 61-62
sketchaway.wordpress.com

Southern-Pearce, Pat 23, 46, 58, 66, 103, 116
Flickr: patsouthern-pearce/Skyeshell

Steel, Liz 65, 100, 103-104
lizsteel.com

Theo, Francis 82
theofrancis.blogspot.sg

Wiltse, Kris 53, 73, 107
kriswiltse.com

Wong, Gail 45, 74, 93
glwsketchworks.blogspot.com